GRINDHOPPING

build a rewarding career
without paying your dues

GRINDHOPPING

build a rewarding career
without paying your dues

Laura Vanderkam

McGraw-Hill

New York   Chicago   San Francisco   Lisbon   London
Madrid   Mexico City   Milan   New Delhi   San Juan
Seoul   Singapore   Sydney   Toronto

1 2 3 4 5 6 7 8 9 0 DOC/DOC 0 9 8 7 6

ISBN-13: 978-0-07-147933-2
ISBN-10:   0-07-147933-3

This publication is designed to provide accurate and authoritative information in regard to the subject matter covered. It is sold with the understanding that neither the author nor the publisher is engaged in rendering legal, accounting, or other professional service. If legal advice or other expert assistance is required, the services of a competent professional person should be sought.
> —*From a Declaration of Principles jointly adopted by Committee of the American Bar Association and a Committee of Publishers.*

McGraw-Hill books are available at special quantity discounts to use as premiums and sales promotions, or for use in corporate training programs. For more information, please write to the Director of Special Sales, McGraw-Hill Professional, Two Penn Plaza, New York, NY 10121-2298. Or contact your local bookstore.

Library of Congress Cataloging-in-Publication Data
Vanderkam, Laura.
  Grindhopping : build a rewarding career without paying your dues / Laura Vanderkam.
      p. cm.
  Includes bibliographical references and index.
  ISBN 0-07-147933-3 (alk. paper)
  1. Self-employed—United States—Handbooks, manuals, etc. 2. Small business—United States—Handbooks, manuals, etc. 3. Self-employed—United States—Case studies. 4. Small business—United States—Case studies. 5. Entrepreneurship—United States—Handbooks, manuals, etc. 6. Entrepreneurship—United States—Case studies. I. Title. II. Title: Build a rewarding career without paying your dues.

HD8037.U5V35 2007
650.1—dc22   2006028911

TABLE OF CONTENTS

INTRODUCTION

Grindhopping \grīnd-häp-ing\ *n* 1. Hopping out of the corporate grind and into the work you want. 2. Building a rewarding career without paying your dues.

When I first started writing this book about Grindhopping, people kept asking me how I coined that word. The truth is that it just came to me one wretched day in August 2005, when absolutely nothing else was going right with my freelance writing work. Editors and sources weren't returning my phone calls. Calling the copy I was cranking out "mush" would, frankly, be undeserved praise.

On the other hand, I was barefoot and wearing comfy jeans at 2 p.m. It was a beautiful summer afternoon. When I mentally checked out for the day, I could pour myself a glass of wine, crack open a book, sit on the balcony, and feel no shame. Hey, I said to myself, at least this isn't the grind. I'm trying to hop over all that photocopying and org chart and office politics nonsense into the life I want. I'm *Grindhopping*. Maybe someone should write a book about that.

But really, although I had lacked a word for the topic before then, my own interest in Grindhopping had begun much earlier—at age four, to be exact. I had just started five-day-a-week nursery school classes. Already the daily grind was getting to me. I remember standing, pigtailed, in line for some school function when a thought popped into my head: Starting then, looking to the future, I would have to get up and go somewhere I was "supposed" to go every day, Monday through Friday, week after week, year after year, until the day I retired. And the thought of that near-life sentence filled my little soul with dread.

I laugh at that now. I was a weird kid. It also wasn't even true in my own experience. In school, you get summers off for good behavior. My mother ran her own home-based tutoring company when my brothers and I were little, which gave her a lot of control over her time. But the fear of the grind stayed with me. I worked at *USA Today* for a year after college. I learned a lot. But since that experience of spending more on pantyhose than on beer, I haven't had a real job. Since 2002, I've been making a living and building a career in other ways.

Like an anthropologist observing a vast, mysterious civilization, though, I'm fascinated by the world of work. I read the *Wall Street Journal* and all the business magazines. I grill my peers about their adventures in making a living. Then I grill them about the hasty retreats back to graduate school that everyone seems to make. What I've discovered is that, while many college career departments try to shoehorn young people into the kinds of careers that look good in the job placement stats, not everyone is easily cubicled. In today's economy, fortunately, you don't need to be.

To write this book, I posted queries on e-mail lists, asked everyone I knew to cough up their contacts, and otherwise tracked down young free spirits across the country. These Grindhoppers, I discovered, are not only having a blast at "work," they aren't living in cardboard boxes, either. None of them has started the next Microsoft, but you don't need to. Starting a one-person wedding photography venture with a sideline in fine photographic art will do. So will designing hip embroidery patterns, or writing about Scotch, or running a surfing camp, or shooting training videos that—oh, the irony!—corporate grinders will be forced to watch. Most Grindhoppers required no start-up capital for their ventures beyond the willingness to take a risk. What these lifestyle entrepreneurs do have in common, though, is that thinking about the daily grind filled them with as much dread as I felt as a pigtailed preschooler.

So they hopped out of it.

Their stories will inspire you to do the same.

GRINDHOPPING

build a rewarding career
without paying your dues

GRINDHOPPING

CARVING YOUR *OWN* CAREER PATH

...from breath mints to worm poop

The first cold morning of the 2005 New York City transit strike, both the potential of the new economy and its reality for many people stood out as starkly for me as Manhattan's towers against the gray sky.

The city's train and bus operators walked off the job on December 20 to keep their old-economy perks of full pensions at age 55 and free health coverage. Few of the white-collar types who were padlocked out of the subways had any of that.

Still, city officials claimed that all the changes in the workplace since 1980 meant that this strike would not snarl commerce like the 11-day crunch 25 years before. Now laptops and Blackberries and cell phones meant that we could be as productive in our jammies as we would be at the office.

Unfortunately, no one told the bundled commuters roving the streets like herds of driven sheep. When the boss says you have to come to work so he can "manage" you, you show up—even if all that commuting just guarantees that you'll be in one place where you can e-mail and call people in *other* places.

Normally, I work from my bedroom. But that day I'd arranged to interview the leaders of Oral Fixation Mints, a profitable start-up whose sleek mint tins had landed in over 1,000 stores in a dozen countries and in the well-photographed hands of celebrities including Carmen Electra and Britney Spears. Since their revenue was growing in double digits every month, I thought they might have some tips for young people looking to carve interesting career paths. I don't live far from Penn Station, so I didn't bother to reschedule. I battled through the commuting crowds and out to the company offices in the historic Chocolate Factory in Hopewell, New Jersey.

I'm not sure what I was expecting. Certainly not cubicles. But as Oral Fix's president, Henry Rich, 25, gave me a tour of the renovated building, I realized that he did *not* have a long commute. He simply got out of bed, stumbled through the band Rich & Royal's recording studio (decorated with an unoccupied birdcage in the shape of a woman that a sculptor friend was storing there), and was, in two seconds, making coffee in the office kitchen.

No suits were likely to be part of that journey. Indeed, none of the Oral Fix executives—Rich, Jeremy Kahn, or COO Eric Lybeck, who moonlights as the Rich & Royal guitarist—appeared to have shaved just because it was Tuesday. The cozy factory-turned-lofts didn't inspire it. Nor did the relaxed décor. A lovely antique music box stood behind the dining room table. Random objects—from a stuffed bear to a sculpture of a watermelon with fangs—were strewn on top of it and every other surface in the place. Jack, the dog, lingered in the toasty second-floor office, unperturbed by the thick scent of peppermint oil, cinnamon, and spearmint oozing from hundreds of mint tins. The rest of us sat downstairs in this cross between grandma's attic and a candy store drinking coffee and yapping about aesthetics, another band called Rackett that Rich and Lybeck had played in with Paul Muldoon (featuring the Pulitzer Prize–winning poet's lyrics), and, yes, Oral Fixation's business story.

After all, it was a Tuesday. We were working.

Kahn and Rich, the tale goes, were punching the clock at a New Jersey wine shop after college when they got to talking about Kahn's habit of smoking during all his breaks. Kahn couldn't give up cigarettes, he told Rich, because he had an "oral fixation." What a great name for a mint company, Rich mused. Since neither was particularly wedded to the wine business, they decided it would be a great name for their mint company. "Let's do it," Kahn said. They shook on it, and thus Oral Fixation Mints was born.

Like the child the stuffed bear was intended for, the venture entered the world screaming and helpless. The wine store owners thought it was "one of the worst ideas they'd ever heard," Rich said. When he and Kahn quit their jobs, their former college classmates laughed. Starting a tech company? Now that people could see. But *candy manufacturing*? A friend invested on the condition of anonymity. Kahn and Rich moved into the upper floor of Rich's loft in the Chocolate Factory and, they joked, Googled "mint making" for one long, revenueless year.

But they got smarter. Rich, who had created his own concentration called "aesthetics" in college, had written his thesis on how beautiful everyday objects could improve people's lives. They decided that their best niche was to create such objects. With the smoking ban in New York City bars taking effect soon, they knew people would be hunting for a still-edgy stand-in. So they designed sleek, minimalist tins that resembled cigarette cases. They brainstormed catchy flavors: Sugar Free Tibet, Mojito Mint, Caffeinated Chai Mints. They hired Lybeck to run the tablet press when he wasn't practicing the guitar. Pretty soon he was managing the guy who ran the tablet press. Then he was calling up the Dr. Seuss-ish mint factory in Chicago and ordering thousands of the things ("Your upward mobility here has been astounding," Rich noted). As long as the tins were cheaper than a cappuccino and cool enough that every hipster who got her hands on them would offer mints to her friends, word of mouth, they hoped, would substitute for the advertising cash they lacked. And with the ability to sell this niche product online, they could meet demand as soon as it grew.

Somehow, it all worked. They landed space in a few high-end retail stores, including various W Hotels and Kate's Paperie. With carefully arranged delivery to dressing rooms, the mints showed up in celebrities' hands (and hence in paparazzi photos) at the Video Music Awards and other shows. Distribution took off. So did Web sales. The team recently hired a national sales director and hunkered down with her to set company goals. Among them: launching new products, and boosting Oral Fix revenue to $2 million a year.

Sitting around the table, the Oral Fix team told me that they had much to celebrate. But they were also introspective about the journey. Running a tablet machine that broke down every time the humidity topped normal had been tough. So was the daily water torture of small retail accounts. On the other hand, all the initial craziness of sprinting to the UPS Store and fixing the dehumidifier while cranking out serious-looking press releases? "We went through that in a year and a half," Rich said. "To climb the corporate ladder takes your whole life."

And he didn't want that. He wanted to be driving a growing, profitable company at age 25 while combining business trips with gigs for his band. "I wanted to do something where I could be my own boss, determine my own fate," he had told me on the phone earlier. "I knew the entrepreneurship track was filled with risk, but I felt a lot more comfortable failing on my own accord than working for someone else and failing at that."

He felt that way even more when he talked to fellow members of his college class of 2002, those who held more traditional jobs in the grind. "A lot of friends left their first jobs really disillusioned," he said. They thought a real job meant gritting their teeth and bearing it. They thought you had to dress up, make a daily commute, do what others told you to, sit in a cubicle, and claw your way to the top. Rich, Kahn, and Lybeck found a secret, buried in their mint tins:

"You don't have to."

MEET THE GRINDHOPPERS

Ah, you may be thinking. Young entrepreneurs with wacky ideas. *Haven't I read this story before?*

It's a tale that was burned on our brains by *Fast Company* cover stories during the dot-com boom. If this were 1997, I'd now write a transition paragraph about how the Oral Fix guys are showing that the old work rules have changed. Employers are finished! It's all about Brand You! I would quote giddy gurus and futurists claiming that technology was empowering all new-economy workers to rise up against our old feudal employer-masters. We would all be free agents and, like the Oral Fix guys, we would not wear ties, darn it. We would bring our birds to work (or at least decorate our offices with birdcages). We would demand the flexibility and work-life balance that would finally smash the glass ceilings that decades of social advances had barely scratched. Every sap with an Internet connection would start a business in her garage (or in her Chocolate Factory loft), and so salaries would soar as employers struggled to find the combo of options, bonuses, and in-cubicle massages that would let them compete.

But I'm writing this in 2006. Half a decade after the dot-com shakeout, the futurists are still nursing a hangover. Plenty of young, would-be free agents tried the start-up life, burned through people's retirement funds, then flocked back to law school or whatever button-down operation would pay them. Judging by the popularity of *Dilbert*, that "rising up against our old feudal employer-masters" thing is a work in progress. Some people, allegedly, have flexible hours, but given the number of folks in suits I saw trudging in the cold that subwayless morning, it's safe to say that the majority of white-collar workers are still working in little cubicle sweatshops from the hours of 9 to 5 or 6 or 7 or whatever.

We're not taking all our vacation days. Downsizing and our own credit card debts have many of us clinging to jobs out of fear of what would happen if we, too, were laid off. The technology that would enable us to work at any place, at any time hasn't lifted us out of the daily grind. It's just let the office follow us home, so that we work every place, all the time, checking our Blackberries on dates and other such horrors. After all, some crisis might come up at work, and we're too insecure in our jobs to let it slide.

"Empowerment" is still an HR buzzword. For most white-collar workers, though, it is not a feature of new-economy life.

In the five years since the Nasdaq crash, I have interviewed scores of young people about their career choices. The subtext of these conversations is that the gurus and futurists were wrong about most people. But they were not wrong about what is *possible* in this new economy.

We are entering a world where, if you are a young person embarking on a white-collar career, you have two almost equally feasible options.

You can start at the entry level and climb up through the *Dilbert* track, with its cubicles and steady paychecks. Some people call this paying your dues.

Certainly, this option seems safer. In this career track, pay is mostly based on tenure. There are job titles, which can help you define your identity. You'll receive regular raises, even if they are small. Your company will provide benefits, even if you do pay more each year for the privilege of carrying mediocre health insurance. There's tech support if your computer breaks down, a place to go to during the day to make you feel productive, and meetings to occupy you, even if you're not sure they're accomplishing much. Sure, in some industries you learn a lot while you're in the grind. Some companies still train their new hires and give them meaningful opportunities that tap their talents. Some, eventually, let you work when and where you choose on fun projects that allow you to execute your authentic vision. But in most cases, you won't experience those joys until you are quite high up the ladder. In the grind, people expect to spend their twenties and early thirties paying their dues. Even traditional schools of thought on entrepreneurship hold that it's better to put in your time when you're young, and wait until you're established to strike out on your own.

Then there is the world of the *Grindhoppers*, young people who don't want to put in years in the grind before achieving career bliss or doing their own thing. They want to hop over the grind from the start. They want to control their lives, working when, where, and how much they want. They want to choose their projects, learn a lot, have fun, and be compensated appropriately for the results they produce. They are often small business entrepreneurs like the Oral Fix guys, although they are also freelancers, consultants, artists, and moonlighters.

> **Grindhoppers understand that the lower levels of most big companies are toxic places for talented, ambitious young people to languish. The politics are bad, the hours worse, the chances for advancement low, and the probability of getting canned before you get anywhere high. And that's if you get in the door in the first place.**

Grindhoppers understand that the lower levels of most big companies are toxic places for talented, ambitious young people to languish. The politics are bad, the hours worse, the chances for advancement low, and the probability of getting canned before you get anywhere high. And that's if you get in the door in the first place.

They also understand that in the real new economy (not the mythical one where everybody brings her bird to work), there is simply more space for young people to carve their own paths far from the mass-market big conglomerates that appear to dominate our world.

Chris Anderson, editor-in-chief of *Wired* magazine, calls this the "Long Tail" aspect of the new economy. He takes the name from a feature of a common statistical distribution curve. High- amplitude or high-frequency data points cluster near the vertical axis; these taper off to low-amplitude or low-frequency points farther out to the right on the curve. These low-amplitude data points look like a long skinny tail, stretching out toward infinity.

They also understand that in the real new economy (not the mythical one where everybody brings her bird to work), there is simply more space for young people to carve their own paths far from the mass-market big conglomerates that appear to dominate our world. 99

Lots of distribution curves feature long tails. For instance, a graph that mapped the number of times a word appeared in this book (the vertical axis) against the rank of that word's usage (the horizontal axis) would take this form. The word *the* is used on every page; it would be right up against the vertical axis with a usage rank of 1, appearing more than 1,000 times. *Mint*, on the other hand, appears far less frequently. We'd find a word like *mint* hugging the horizontal axis out at a word rank in the hundreds, or higher, appearing just a few times.

Individually, these infrequent words like *mint* do not take up much space in *Grindhopping*. However, one of the most interesting features of the long-tail curve is that if you add up the usage of all these infrequent words (calculating the space under the tail), they're likely to take up as much room in this book, collectively, as the most common words like *a, and, the, in, of,* and *to.* Long tails slither out for a long, long way.

So what does this statistics lesson, with a twist of calculus, have to do with building a career? In the past, businesses survived by being big enough to reach big markets. Because the cost of keeping products on hand in physical stores, and of keeping full-time employees on hand to provide services, is high, businesses had to offer mass products to satisfy mass tastes. That's the head of the statistical distribution curve (where *the* would be in a plot of word use in this book).

But these businesses were missing out on great opportunities. Just as words like *mint* and *chocolate* collectively appear as many times as *the* or *a*, the market for niche products and services has always had just as much potential as the market for mass products and services. The problem was that, in the past, it was simply too expensive to serve customers who wanted those things. There would only be a handful of such niche lovers in any given physical location. An Austin-based woman who wanted to run a business doing embroidery portraits might find only a few takers in her town. That's hardly enough cash to keep her register ringing.

Now, though, since technology makes it as easy and cheap for an embroidery connoisseur in Beverly Hills to find and hire our Austin-based artist as it would be if she were down the street, niche products and services for niche markets can translate into decent results.

That means that the economy can support more microbusinesses out under the long tail now than at any point in the past. You don't have to work for Wrigley's, it turns out, to make a living selling mints. These days, you can find a market for just about anything you want to do, and you need very little money to do it.

So Grindhoppers use the more fluid nature of the modern, wired economy to hop over the low rungs of big institutions and do their own thing out under the market's long tail. Technology and the new economy do make that possible for them, more than for any previous generation. Grindhoppers look at all this new space in the economic universe and realize that if they're willing to forgo a bit of safety, they can have the life they want whenever they are able to handle it.

This book is about them. It shows how dozens of young people have built careers without paying their dues in big companies—and how you can, too.

THE NEW-ECONOMY SPLIT

Having scrupulously avoided getting a real job through my twenties, I wasn't aware of how little the advent of the new economy had changed the lives of most white-collar workers until I came across a tattered copy of William H. Whyte's *Organization Man* a few months ago. This 1956 tome documented how modern American white-collar workers were willing to give up control of their destinies for the safety and collegial vibe of large institutions.

I bought my copy for $1 in a Muncie, Indiana, used bookstore. That's a 1950s price, but after reading former General Electric CEO Jack Welch's 2005 book, *Winning*, I decided that the price tag and the male pronouns were the only things in Whyte's opus that couldn't have been written last year.

What happens when a bright, ambitious, free-spirited young man tries to fit in with a big company? Whyte asks. He won't find kindred spirits. "Trainees," Whyte writes of young workers, "hope to rise high and hope just as much not to suffer the personal load of doing so. Frequently they talk of finding a sort of plateau—a position well enough up to be interesting but not so far up as to have one's neck outstretched for others to chop at."

The typical young Organization Man does not incline to a smaller firm, Whyte writes: "It may offer opportunity but it offers it too soon. By contrast, big business . . . will defer opportunity until he is ready for it." In the meantime, the man companies decide they need is a practical "team-player fellow."

Yes, *team player* was a buzzword in 1956, too.

But certainly big organizations could still find room for a quirky overachiever, right? Whyte asked a group of young GE workers what they would do if a lone genius type applied for a job. "After some thought, a few trainees said they thought maybe he could work out; because of the fraternity-like life of the training program, they 'could iron out his rough spots.' Others disagreed; the man would be too hopelessly antisocial to remold. 'I don't think we would put up with a fellow like that now,' one said."

"I would sacrifice brilliance," he quotes another young man as saying, "for human understanding every time."

Jack Welch started working at GE at about the same time, in the early 1960s, and, judging by his book, GE still has the same policies in place. In *Winning*, he talks about James, an "extremely smart and capable employee" brought in from a top-tier consulting firm. "We figured at least three GE businesses would be fighting over him within six months."

Alas, "A year came and went and no one would touch him. I couldn't figure out why until I sat in on his first performance review with his boss and the HR team. There I learned that James came into the office at ten or eleven each day and left late, at 8:00 p.m. or so." Those were plenty of hours, Welch notes, except that other people liked to schedule meetings at 8:00 a.m. "But James didn't seem to care about GE's routines. He had his own way of doing things."

This being a morality tale, the ending is as simple as the prose: "He had to leave the company." Today's big organizations, just like the 1950s Organization, won't put up with a fellow like that.

In addition to warning readers not to become a "James," Welch instructs modern young fellows in all sorts of other play-by-the-rules concepts that favor the Organization over their own happiness. We must beware of "gaps" on our résumés. We shouldn't quit bad jobs before we find other jobs because of those gaps. If we have bad bosses, the first place to look for an explanation is our own performance—or our attitude: "It just might be that the source of your problem with your boss is that you are, at your core, a boss hater. . . . Boss haters usually exude constant low-level negativity toward 'the system,' and when they do, their bosses feel it, and they return the favor."

Yes, Welch tells us, there are no "shortcuts" to getting promoted (translation: don't think about job hopping or doing free agency stints to speed up the process). As for work-life balance, well, that's only for people who've put in enough face time to let the organization know them. They've proven themselves to be Organization Men.

Since *Fortune* called Welch the "manager of the century," I'm inclined to believe that much of the professional world follows his rules. Despite the layoffs and pension explosions of the past two decades, many white-collar workers still utter the creed Whyte spelled out in his book, written five decades ago:

> *Be loyal to the company and the company will be loyal to you. After all, if you do a good job for the organization, it is only good sense for the organization to be good to you, because that will be best for everybody.*

We know on some level that this isn't true. In 2001, for instance, *USA Today* fired three sports reporters, with over 50 years' experience between them, for writing "Kilroy was here" in what appeared to be dust on the sculpture outside the CEO's office. (It turned out to be part of the installation. The artist herself said it was repairable.)

But the new-economy worker, like the old-economy worker, doesn't like to think about that too much. She fears outstretched neck–chopping possibilities. She prefers human understanding to brilliance. She wants to be taken care of. For all the books out there claiming that the new economy would make us all free agents, many white-collar workers are so unable to take control of their destinies that they need automatic 401(k) enrollment in order to save. The new-economy worker, like the old-economy worker, grew up changing classes when a bell rang in school. She showed up and did her assignments, even if all she learned was that getting somewhere in life required appearing in the same place, Monday through Friday, and doing what other people said she should do.

It's a habit that the new-economy worker is scared to drop as a grown-up, even if a transit strike means that she has to hike three miles in the snow to get to work.

I was reminded of this in a recent *Time* magazine profile of Best Buy, still one of the few companies to try that new-economy "inevitability" of a work-whenever-and-wherever policy at headquarters. As long as the work gets done, Best Buy said, who cares about face time?

Like James's managers at GE, it turned out, a lot of employees cared. Traci Tobias in travel noted, "There was a lot of trepidation. . . . A lot of, Can I really do this? Do I need to stop and tell someone? What will people think of me?" Switching the Minneapolis headquarters to a "results-oriented work environment" required baby steps, *Time* noted. One department asked people to post where they would be on a calendar—like a teacher granting hall passes—until they got into the habit of believing that you actually didn't have to be anywhere.

Corporate strategist Denise LaMere confessed that she wasn't sure how she could prove herself at the new Best Buy. "It made me nervous," the article quotes her as saying. Since she didn't have children, she had gotten ahead by always being the first one in and the last one out.

"I had all this panic," she said. "Everything we knew about success was suddenly changing."

She thought success was about being the first one in and the last one out. It's a totally different view of the universe from the one the Oral Fix guys have, where success is getting results, living the life you want, and not letting yourself be judged on metrics that don't matter. As Rich puts it, "If you ever took a pass-fail class in college, and still worked really hard, you can run your own business."

The average worker, on the other hand, expects a grade, just like she earned as a child.

It's not a generation thing. Best Buy's Tobias and LaMere were both under 40 at the time the article was written. That's where the boom stories went wrong. What the futurists saw as a fundamental shift turned out, instead, to be early evidence of a split.

We all inhabit the same white-collar career universe, but there are two ways of dealing with it. After all, the same world that keeps

LaMere fretting about the definition of success found a way to get Oral Fixation mints into Britney Spears's purse. Technology wound up enabling a split, not a shift.

Grindhoppers, for instance, use e-mail as a leveling tool. People will read your e-mails who would never take your calls. For others, though, e-mail has meant increasing the grind's control over your life. Now your boss expects you to read and complete the assignment he sent you, via Blackberry, at 8 p.m.

I see evidence of the split in Barbara Ehrenreich's book *Bait and Switch: The (Futile) Pursuit of the American Dream*. Ehrenreich created a fake white-collar identity so that she could go undercover and shine so bright a light on the cubicle world that the corporate beast would squint. There was just one problem: after looking for 10 months and spending thousands of dollars on career consultants operating, practically, out of their living rooms, she couldn't get a job.

A Grindhopper would look at that situation and decide that the smartest course of action would be to become one of those career coaches. But Ehrenreich just rants that it is unfair that people go to college, get jobs, play by the rules, get canned anyway, and then, when they post their résumés on the Internet, don't immediately land long-term jobs in their fields with good wages and benefits.

Grindhoppers, on the other hand, don't think anyone owes them the perfect job. They realize that if they want the perfect job, no one is stopping them from creating it.

> **Grindhoppers don't think anyone owes them the perfect job. They realize that if they want the perfect job, no one is stopping them from creating it.**

They refuse to put their destinies in someone else's hands. They've crossed the divide between "safe" and "I choose" in their minds. Once you decide to become a Grindhopper, you become as evangelical as any new convert. When I wrote a piece called "The Sanity of Self-Employment" for *USA Today* in July 2004, I was deluged with tales from young free agents who were happy that someone saw their decision to forgo the grind the same way they did—as a smart career move for people who look at the corporate world's lower ranks and think, "I can do better." When I started doing interviews for this book, I was amazed at how long people wanted to prattle on about the joy of doing what you love, and the happiness that comes from working on your own terms.

I'm still amazed every time I see the phone bill.

Unfortunately, there aren't a lot of career-building guides out there for young Grindhoppers. Older organization types warn you to play it safe. As one young woman told me, her father "wants me to go to business school, to work my way up, to get more experience. (I feel starting a business is the best experience I could get.) He feels I don't know enough to start a business. (I think, I'm not going to learn it in the corporate world.) He's afraid I'll fail. (I think failing could be more valuable than two years in business school.) He wants me to be secure. (And like most people my age, I don't think anything's secure anymore.)"

Likewise, most entrepreneurship books are for mid-career professionals who are sick of the grind, not young people who want to build their careers without experiencing it in the first place. Most of them assume that you want to start the next Microsoft, so they talk about writing business plans, borrowing capital, and meeting with venture capitalists (VCs). They don't take into account microbusinesses, freelancing, consulting, and other forms of free agency that don't require much funding or incorporation. None of these books talks about using free agency as a tool to get where you want to be professionally. Many Grindhoppers are willing to reenter the corporate world later in life, when they're offered interesting projects and positions with real autonomy. These Grindhoppers simply want to hop over the lower levels of the grind. Few books tell you how to build your life to reach the projects and responsibilities you deserve as soon as possible.

So this book aims to fill the gap. While Grindhoppers are an elite, gutsy group, their ranks are growing. The National Association for the Self-Employed reports that "Over time, there . . . has been a trend toward younger workers entering self-employment." A recent NASE survey found that 13.9 percent of its membership was under 35 years old. Bureau of Labor Statistics figures show that about 10 million Americans are unincorporated and self-employed; another 4 million independent workers (roughly) have incorporated. Daniel Pink, author of *Free Agent Nation*, estimates that there are another 13 million microbusinesses in America that don't show up in the self-employed count. If 13.9 percent of these 27 million or so free agents are under 35, that means that 3.75 million folks in their twenties and early thirties call themselves boss. Small business owners—those who have moved outside the microbusiness range—add thousands more to that total. Many others who are currently working for companies have used free agent gigs in the past to launch themselves into higher spots on the ladder.

These four million or so young people are sick of being offered career books that tell them that they should hold a big organization job for a year to show stability, and that gaps in official employment on their résumés are the career equivalent of telling potential sex partners that you have an STD.

Grindhoppers know that by the time you're sending a résumé to HR, you're toast. They don't believe in following arbitrary rules. When they see that you need 12 years to be a midlevel partner in a law firm, that you need to spend two years answering phones at a magazine to move up to an editing job, that you need to put in years of organization time at a candy manufacturing company to make decisions about design, taste, and markets, they take that as a challenge.

I have the skills I need now, they say, or I can learn them faster than anyone will notice what I lack.

After interviewing these Grindhoppers, I've discovered that they live by a different set of career rules:

1 **Always be your own boss.**
2 **Know where you're going.**
3 **Recalculate risk.**
4 **Think projects, not jobs.**
5 **Seek to be judged on results (and deliver them).**
6 **Everything is negotiable.**
7 **Cultivate a network and a nimble mind.**

The next seven chapters will show how Grindhoppers build these guidelines into their lives. Then, before I finish up with a Cliff Notes version of this book and a plug for the Web site, we'll look at some of the downsides to this sort of life. There are a few, but they're not nearly as bad as folks in the grind make them out to be. Sometimes people like to justify their own lives by telling you it's a horrible decision to strike out on your own. They repeat misleading statistics about how many small businesses fail in order to discourage you. Likewise, plenty of books for young folks by self-appointed Generational Spokespeople will tell you that it's just too hard to build a good life in this difficult, difficult world that the baby boomers have stacked against you. We are *Strapped*, to quote one recent title. We are *Generation Debt*, to quote another, discovering in the subtitle *Why Now Is a Terrible Time to Be Young*. We are caught up in a *Quarterlife Crisis*, unable to translate our concentration in aesthetics into an actual, career-boosting position.

Nonsense. For all the complaining, there has never been an easier time to build a career doing what you love. You do not have to hate your first job. Technology and the openness in the new economy are pushing us toward a world where there are no limits on what ambitious young workers can earn or do.

While plenty of nervous 20-somethings spend years finding themselves in unfocused career feints or in the endless degree programs they flee to when they learn that life is not like school, Grindhoppers tackle the world differently. They know that you can build a great career without mucking through the grind. They know that you can have the life you choose without waiting until you are older—in short, without paying your dues.

> **"While plenty of nervous 20-somethings spend years finding themselves in unfocused career feints or in the endless degree programs they flee to when they learn that life is not like school, Grindhoppers tackle the world differently. They know that you can build a great career without mucking through the grind. They know that you can have the life you choose without waiting until you are older—in short, without paying your dues."**

THE JOY OF WORK

Like the Oral Fix headquarters, the TerraCycle factory in Trenton, New Jersey, lacks the sophistication that places obsessed with organization charts tend to finance.

Staring out the train window on the way there, I kept noticing plastic soda bottles wedged into the snow along the tracks. Then I met Tom Szaky, the 23-year-old CEO of this eco-friendly fertilizer company, and realized that he would have paid me good money to dump that trash in his office. In the TerraCycle world, used soda bottles become plant food bottles. Once they slap on a shrink-wrap label, you barely notice that the bottles that used to be Sprite are green and the reincarnated Coke and Pepsi bottles are clear. (I can hear GE's Six Sigma black belts chanting, "Variation is evil" and smiting themselves on their foreheads right now.)

While TerraCycle has plenty of use for trash, the company doesn't have any use for big-company pretensions. The day I visited, a *Wall Street Journal* article announced that archcompetitor Scotts Miracle-Gro planned to fire any employee who persisted in smoking after a certain deadline that fall. Szaky got a good laugh out of that one. "You can smoke," he said, gesturing outside. I've never visited Miracle-Gro's headquarters, but I'm guessing that they aren't covered with chipped green paint, and that the windows don't feature blinds that are bent at key places. Nor are they perched on a dead-end street close to an auto-impounding lot in a city where a bullet once went through the CEO's bedroom window.

But Szaky has always had to do things cheaply. A Hungarian immigrant to the United States via Canada, he dropped out of college at age 19 to start this company. He got the idea after becoming entranced with a worm composting machine he saw on a visit to Montreal. He bought one and hit up university dining halls for their garbage. He pushed the resulting concoction into a few organic stores. After some rough starts, sales rose faster than the worms could eat. He had to buy equipment to expand, which caused the company's bank account to go from six figures to nothing several times.

Perhaps because of that roller coaster, the company wastes nothing. As Szaky showed me around the plant's steaming vats of worm "castings" (that's an industry euphemism; he prefers "worm poop"), I realized that the benefit of locating a factory in a place like Trenton is that the local labor force is loyal and cheap. About half a dozen workers bustled around the delivery and packing areas; a team of five workers listened to headphones as they stripped labels off soda bottles in the back. In addition to reusing soda bottles, TerraCycle takes delivery of spray nozzles that other companies want to cast off. Even the boxes tend to be misprinted ones that some other company is trying to dump.

That will change soon, though. Wal-Mart doesn't allow vendors to use repurposed boxes, and TerraCycle just landed a contract to sell bottles of the fertilizer in Wal-Mart's U.S. stores. With that and Home Depot distribution, Szaky plans to sell $3 million or so of the product this year. That's based on up-front capital of half a year's college tuition.

And a lot of worm poop.

It's a charming story: "Entrepreneur, 23, Turns Crap into Cash." That grabber's not lost on Szaky. "Dropping out of college—that's fantastic," he told me, referring to his biography. "The press helped make this company." Indeed, the walls featured dozens of clippings (possibly covering the chipped paint).

More seriously, though, "There are a lot of perks being young in this," he told me. "You're allowed to screw up, screw up, screw up and no one will hold it against you." You can get any high-level person to talk with you by pushing the youth factor, though Szaky doesn't downplay persistence. He called Wal-Mart "basically every half hour" until it agreed to look at his wares. But hey, "anything is possible" when you're young. "You haven't been proven wrong."

That's good for Szaky, who cringes at the thought of spending his days in a suit, or spending years in a manufacturing organization before he could make decisions about how a factory should run. He wanted to avoid the grind so much that he started six companies that didn't work before he lit on the TerraCycle idea. A lot of people, Szaky told me, look at their particular skills and ask, "Where can I get the most money to execute that skill?' But that's a tough line to walk versus asking 'what do I enjoy doing?' and doing that."

That's the Grindhopper creed: do what you love, and even if it all blows up six times before the seventh one takes, you won't have wasted time. Bullet through the window or not, Szaky said, "I don't consider this work at all.'

GRINDHOPPING
GUIDELINE #1:

ALWAYS BE YOUR OWN BOSS
No compromises, no excuses

"Best things about running a business? No sucking up to the boss, no watering down of your ideas and vision. If you know what you want and are willing to give it a try, you can just move forward with it."
—Jenny Hart, owner and founder of Sublime Stitching

O f all the guidelines, "always be your own boss" is the one that Grindhoppers most take to heart. A Grindhopper will not compromise her picture of the ideal career and life for long. She runs the show, just as a boss would. She also allows herself no excuses for failing to achieve that ideal, just as a boss would allow her no excuses.

This combination of independence and self-discipline is rare. But if you've got them both—or can cultivate them—you can build a career without paying your dues, and feel more bliss at work than most people think is possible.

That's what a group of young female entrepreneurs called the Austin Craft Mafia is doing.

Tina Lockwood, one of the Mafia ringleaders, grew up sewing in her bedroom at night, altering the clothes her mother bought at Kmart to match her own sense of style. She made skirts out of T-shirts. She embroidered belts. She tried to look like a rock star. Indeed, in college at Southwest Texas State University, she played guitar in a band called Search for Saturnalia. She loved the music, but she didn't like the plain-vanilla guitar straps she found at stores. So she made her own red-and-white-striped one with cherries on it and modeled her creation at concerts.

Other "lady rock stars," as Lockwood calls her customers, saw the strap and wanted copies. She dutifully sewed and sold them and a few more crafty items on the side. A friend who wrote for *Jane* magazine saw some wall hangings Lockwood designed that incorporated vintage clothing, and published a piece on how to create your own. Lockwood set up a Web site to capture any business that came out of that publicity. Orders came in. Sparkle Craft, as she called her venture, seemed like a reasonable proposition.

But as the first person in her family to graduate from college, Lockwood felt pressure to get a "real" job. She landed a research position at a company that did work for high-tech outfits. She pulled together PowerPoint presentations on things like servers, routers, microprocessors, and home computers.

It was a good job. The money was good. She was promoted quickly. She liked her coworkers. There was, of course, the "boss thing." (I couldn't help noticing that she scrunched her shoulders every time she talked about working for someone else.) But who does like having a boss? No one seemed to mind that she moonlighted running Sparkle Craft while she worked at the research firm. She had a bright career ahead of her.

And yet . . . she couldn't ignore the little voice reminding her that she felt more excited about pulling together her outfits in the morning to go to work than she did about the work itself. "I feel happiness when I think about clothes," she told me. "Routers and servers didn't bring me happiness." With orders piling up, she resented taking time away from her passion to do her job. She realized that her passion might have to become her full-time job if she wanted to live a life that made her authentically happy. She might have to become her own boss and take charge of her own career. Given the money she was making, that was a scary thought.

But it was also wildly liberating.

Two of her friends in Austin, Jenny Hart and Jennifer Perkins, were tiptoeing toward the same conclusion around the same time. Hart grew up coloring outside the lines; even as a fourth grader, she told me, she once rebelled against an art project that required her to treat perspective in a way she didn't like. She took up embroidery in 2000 while helping care for her mother during an illness. Like

Lockwood altering her clothes to suit, Hart bristled against the old-fashioned patterns of bonnets and bunnies that craft stores assumed women wanted. After returning to her archival job at an Austin museum, she started daydreaming about shaking up the embroidery industry a (much welcome) bit.

Perkins also spent a lot of time daydreaming. She got a job as an executive assistant right out of college. Then her boss left. She never got another one. She never got fired, either. She had no work beyond the occasional request to fax something. She hung there in job limbo, so bored that she spent hours daily hunting on eBay for vintage stuff that she could incorporate into the jewelry she was building at night. She hawked her big, bold creations in a 'zine called *Naughty Secretary Club* that she also started to kill time.

These three young women kept meeting to gush about their crafts, their big plans, and the inevitable watering down of those plans that working day jobs required. How long could they live with these compromises?

They didn't have long to find out. *Bust* magazine featured Perkins's jewelry in an article. The orders flooded in so fast that she couldn't keep working. She quit and devoted herself full-time to pushing her wares. Soon Naughty Secretary Club designs were being featured everywhere from *Elle Girl* to *Playgirl*. The Do-It-Yourself (DIY) cable network learned about her work and tapped her to host a show called *Craft Lab* (as I'm writing this, it's scheduled to air daily in fall 2006).

Hart got laid off. Far from being upset, she grinned from ear to ear as her boss told her. "You're making my dreams come true!" she thought. Losing her job gave her the push she needed to start an embroidery pattern business that she called Sublime Stitching. Now Hart spends her days designing renegade patterns and hawking them on her Web site. Forget bonnets and bunnies. Her kits include sushi roll patterns, patterns that look like tattoos, and still others of wrestling pens. The embroidery industry hasn't known quite what to make of her, but young hip crafters snatch the patterns up. Hart also taps her fine art training by taking commissions to embroider portraits of her various celebrity fans' friends. Actress Carrie Fisher, for instance, commissioned a portrait of her daughter to give to her mother, a portrait of Tracey Ullman's son to give to Ullman, and a pillow portrait of Elizabeth Taylor's dog, Sugar, which a *W* magazine spread captured perched on Dame Elizabeth's bed.

Lockwood, watching her friends, likewise decided that she was done with measuring the fabric of her life. She was ready to cut.

She quit her job. She read books on marketing at night and took to entrepreneurship like sparkles to clothes. She developed a following of folks who saw her work in publications and online. They loyally linked to her. Around the time I interviewed Lockwood, Sparkle Craft was coming up third when you typed "guitar straps" into Google. These days, she spends her working hours in a pink-painted office in Austin that teems with bolts of fabric. Dozens of decorated guitar straps hang next to spools of brightly colored thread. Hot pink stars adorn most of the other surfaces. When I visited, she was nearly swimming in white fabric flowers, hand-stitched to be sewn on a custom wedding dress order. The dress skirt was hot pink, too—perfect for another lady rocker who wanted to strut down the aisle in style. For someone enamored with clothes, the setup is just about paradise compared to the tech research job. She even changed her last name to "Sparkles" to reflect her new life ("I thought it would be cool to have a clothing line with my name," she says).

These three ladies and six other female craft entrepreneurs in Austin banded together as the "Austin Craft Mafia" to pool money for advertising. As a unified public relations force, they've scored great exposure, including a group show called *Stylelicious*, also on the DIY network.

Along the way, they've discovered that the watering down of authentic ideas and vision that most of us think a job necessitates is a vestige of thinking that someone else should be your boss. When you're stuck in that mindset, you assume that there will be parts of your career that you don't like. You assume that there will be parts that make you unhappy, trade-offs, or things you can't control. When you decide to be your own boss, those things disappear. You can embrace your free spirit, and surround her with as much fabric and sparkles as her heart desires.

The ladies of the Austin Craft Mafia were crafty kids. They got back to that authentic vision by asking two questions. Namely:

···⟫ **When I was a kid, what did I want to be when I grew up (i.e., what do I love so much that I'd do it for free)?**

···⟫ **How can I get people to pay me to create that vision?**

When you talk to people who have found answers to those questions, you notice that they can't contain the joy in their voices. That joy isn't limited to the wealthy or well connected, by the way. No member of the Austin Craft Mafia had to take out huge loans to start her business. Hart, for instance, financed Sublime Stitching with a $1,000 loan from her parents. No Mafia member needed VC financing to fulfill her dreams. In the new economy, you don't need capital and experience to become your own boss. You just have to be ambitious. You have to be impatient and convinced that someone will pay for what your free spirit longs to do. On her last day at her real job, Tina Lockwood Sparkles kept thinking, "My world is open." There was no need to hunch her shoulders anymore.

PICTURING THE IDEAL LIFE

When you are your own boss, you control your life. That means you get to dream up what you'll do with it. Some people are blessed with knowing this and following it from day one. Others of us get caught up in other things. We get confused about our callings. This can be a source of considerable angst. We listen to people who tell us that plastics is the industry of the future. We hear that to find the right job, in Jack Welch's words,

> *You endure the same gummy, time-consuming, up-and-down, iterative process that all working people go through. You take one job, discover what you like and don't like about it and what you're good and bad at, and then, in time, change jobs to get something closer to the right fit. And you do that until one day you realize—hey, I'm finally in the right job. I like what I'm doing, and I'm making the trade-offs I'm willing to make. Yes, trade-offs, because very few jobs are perfect.*

We accept that we'll have to make money creating PowerPoint slides about computers, even though we'd rather sew crazy guitar straps. We'll have to work as secretaries to support our jewelry-making passion, because who on earth would think it's a reasonable goal to get paid to host a craft-making cable TV show?

When you were a kid, though, you didn't think about these things. That's why the "What did you want to be when you grew up?" question is so simply brilliant. This question will save you big bucks on career coaching and a potential midlife crisis.

So find some quiet, meditative time. Then think. When you were a kid, what kind of toys did you play with all day? What books did you hoard from the library? When you daydreamed in class, what did you doodle in your notebooks? Look through old photo albums. Go back through the boxes of stuff your sainted mother has been keeping in the attic because you're too sentimental to throw them out. I shivered when I read a story in a book called *Career Bliss* by Joanne Gordon about a middle-aged woman who'd struggled to realize that she wanted to be a librarian. After becoming one, she discovered a box of her old Nancy Drew books. "As I leafed through the pages, I noticed that as a kid I'd pasted paper pockets and mock checkout cards on the inside front covers," the woman told Gordon. "I'd completely forgotten that when I was young, I pretended to work in a library. Apparently, a part of me never forgot."

What do you love so much that you used to do it for free, like this librarian?

That, quite simply, is what you should do with your life.

Most of the Grindhoppers I interviewed for this book told me that they showed a knack for their professions early on. Not all did. Some started businesses when the opportunity presented itself. A friend asked them to join. The industry was hot. Someone else was selling equipment at a fire-sale price. Many of these Grindhoppers ultimately decided to sell their businesses and look for the next venture. They were trying to get closer to the right fit via the process that Welch described. Some liked this serial entrepreneurship; others told me that it became a bit of a grind over time, too. Anything can become a grind if you let it. That's why I recommend asking the when-I-grow-up question.

> **Grindhoppers who hit the jackpot from the start have not just talent, but affection for their work. They love their work like they'd love a childhood playmate. They do not believe that they should be anything but blissfully happy with their jobs.**

Grindhoppers who hit the jackpot from the start have not just talent, but affection for their work. They love their work like they'd love a childhood playmate. They do not believe that they should be anything but blissfully happy with their jobs.

24

Of course, plenty of career guidebooks tell you to ask the question of what you wanted to be when you grew up. But they approach the question from the perspective that you will have a boss, not that you will be your own boss. So the authors tell you to research "real" job tracks that tap the skills and passions your eight-year-old self possessed. For instance, if you were always putting on shows for people as a kid, the career books say you might do well in sales. Maybe you liked putting on shows about doctors and hospitals. Even better—pharmaceutical sales!

The career books do not tell you to start a theater troupe devoted to medical drama.

I understand why. There are dozens of pharmaceutical companies that are willing to pay you to sell drugs for them. Starting a theater troupe, writing material, luring other actors, landing gigs, and finding backers sounds like a lot of work. Only a very ambitious person could succeed at such a venture. This is why career books don't push entrepreneurship as a default option for people with out-of-the-box career aspirations. Also, the career experts point out, children don't know the range of potential jobs in the economy. They know that there are bakers and actors and gardeners and the guys on the radio Mom plays in the car, but they don't know about senior account managers, unless Mom is one. It's like asking seventh graders to pick stocks. They'll buy only Pepsi and Nike, because these are the brands they see in their middle school lives.

On the other hand, as Peter Lynch showed in his 1993 book *Beating the Street*, a group of seventh graders choosing stocks they've heard of is quite likely to beat money managers favoring "the inexplicable venture that loses money."

Likewise, I recently came across an Oregon-based company called VocationVacations. Started in 2004 by Brian Kurth, a one-time senior account manager type who saw his father go to work, day after day, decade after decade, in an insurance job he hated, this company arranges for folks to spend a few days working with a mentor in the vacationer's dream job. Kurth has a list of available "dream job" vacations on the Web site. From cheese maker to horse trainer to bike shop owner, I'd say that about 90 percent are job titles the under-12 set would recognize.

Maybe the kids are onto something. Even if they don't know what a senior account manager does.

Kurth's primary customers are baby boomers who are bored with their jobs and want to test the waters before they think about a career change. Many have received vacation gift certificates from loved ones who are sick of seeing them suffer in a job that's just a living. So these middle-aged folks take a break from their senior account manager jobs and spend a week making cheese. Then they write testimonials saying, as one man did, "I was in heaven."

Grindhoppers don't want to wait for a vacation at age 50 to be in job heaven. Someone, they know, has these dream careers from the get-go. Somebody didn't have to compromise his desires in order to make a living. Someone is talented and ambitious enough to build these dream careers, and Grindhoppers know that *they* are talented and ambitious. So *this* career book tells you not to dismiss the medical theater troupe idea out of hand.

I'll also go ahead and tell you that entrepreneurship needs to be your default option if you're dreaming of an offbeat career. You may not stay in the entrepreneurial world forever. Plenty of Grindhoppers reenter the corporate world once they're tapped for positions that offer them real autonomy and the chance to execute their authentic vision. But you will have to launch your career that way. While starting a profitable medical theater troupe isn't the kind of venture that's highly likely to succeed, you're even less likely to find someone else who will employ you in such a fashion straight out of school. Someday, after years of running your own troupe, you might be lured into leading an existing acting company with a big budget and an established audience. Then you can direct that troupe toward a medically oriented repertoire. But in the meantime, you're better off doing your own thing if you've got crazy career dreams.

Even dream jobs with real career tracks, like the librarian's, may require more trade-offs than you're willing to make if you work for someone else. Gordon's *Career Bliss* notes that the librarian wanted to work with children. But then she got stuck in the generalist library graduate school program, not the children's one, and she couldn't switch tracks. She worked in the young adult section of a public library after graduation, but her hours of 8:30 to 5:00 didn't bring her into contact with many actual schoolchildren. She investigated working in a public school library, but learned she'd need a teaching certificate to do so. Exasperated and unwilling to go back to school again, she found a private day school that had a run-down, practically budgetless library. No matter. She decided that "the library would be my little kingdom." She applied for outside funding and rebuilt the thing from scratch. Grindhoppers might not be willing to put in so many years of schooling and dues paying to, in essence, build a library themselves. They're the folks who collect books from friends and jet off to Ghana to start a library in an area without one, and hence where people don't care so much about their credentials.

But, like the librarian, they listen to that inner voice. There's no point wasting time ignoring it. There's no bonus virtue gained by doing work you don't love. Before you knew about compromises and trade-offs, you wanted to do something with your life. Grindhoppers realize that when you're young, compromises and trade-offs don't have to enter the equation.

THE MONEY QUESTION

Before anyone whines about that last statement, let me say that I know that bosses don't just choose projects. They also mind the bottom line. Unless you're independently wealthy, building a career without paying your dues requires income. Smart Grindhoppers take the answer to the "What did I want to be when I grew up?" question, and ask, "*How* can I get someone to pay me to do that?"

But they do not ask, "*Can* I get someone to pay me to do that?"

It's an important distinction. If you compromise your authentic vision—choosing pharmaceutical sales instead of starting the theater troupe—you won't be happy. You'll be making trade-offs. Trade-offs make work feel like a grind.

Fortunately, the modern, wired economy has room for ventures that would have seemed ridiculous a few years ago.

Here, it's worth taking a brief detour through economic history.

For all the past century's worship of big business, it has not always been that way. Once upon a time, if you wanted a career in business, either you worked in someone else's home office as a butcher, baker, or candlestick maker, or you worked in your own. Stories of individual entrepreneurs from the colonial era are tough to find, but they do exist. One of the most interesting is that of Elizabeth Murray, whose tale is told by historian Patricia Cleary in the book *Elizabeth Murray: A Woman's Pursuit of Independence in Eighteenth-Century America.*

Around 1749, 23-year-old Murray faced the question of what to do with her life. She wasn't married at the time, and she didn't want to live with relatives. So she needed to find a job. Born in the Scottish borderlands, she considered learning the shopkeeper's trade in London. But London's apprentice laws and traditions were strict; custom dictated that she would have to work in someone else's dress shop for years in order to establish herself. The American colonies, where she'd lived as a teenager, were more accepting of anyone who wanted to hang a shingle and sell her wares. Murray, frankly, liked the idea of skipping the grind and being her own boss. So she decided to open a clothing store in Boston.

As a woman, Murray had trouble arranging credit in her own name; her brother wound up signing for her. After that, though, London's dealers let her import goods in advance of payment. She took out ads in the Boston newspaper announcing her "Capuchins, flower'd Velvet and Capuchin Silks, black Fringes, Bone Lace, a variety of brocaded striped and cross'd bar'd Stuffs and Poplins for Winter Gowns . . ." and enough other bits of fabric to keep Tina Sparkles of Sparkle Craft happy forever. All would be sold "cheap for the cash."

When sales were thin at the store, Murray gave sewing lessons. But she rarely had to resort to moonlighting. Her store did well (so well that Murray had one of her husbands sign a prenuptial agreement) until the American Revolution made importing British goods a dicey proposition.

According to Cleary, Murray was one of at least 90 women entrepreneurs who kept shops in Boston between 1740 and the Revolution. "As partners or patrons of one another's businesses, Boston's workingwomen shared personal and professional ties," Cleary writes. They tapped each other to employ their relatives and supply goods. They provided start-up capital for each sister's business. They bounced ideas off each other. One woman even left her estate to another in her will. These "she-merchants" of Boston reveled in being their own bosses, especially in a world that let men boss women around in other spheres of life.

Men, likewise, ran thousands of small businesses at the dawn of the American experiment. The rise of industrial equipment in the 1800s, though, started a grand consolidation of the butchers, bakers, and candlestick makers of the colonial period into the Tyson Foods, Pepperidge Farms, and GEs of the modern world. The means of production in an industrial economy were too big and expensive for mere mortals to own. As the average business got bigger, popular imagination believed that you had to be a superhuman like Henry Ford or Andrew Carnegie to chart your own course. The rest of us went to work for big organizations—the government, the universities, the corporations, even the big religious denominations.

We got used to having bosses. We got used to having bosses who had bosses. We heard of some great coaches whom we'd happily go into battle for. Unfortunately, I, personally, have also been e-mailed a lot of tales of micromanaging bosses, abusive bosses who throw the mail at you because it was stamped wrong, incompetent bosses who omit crucial bits of information, bullying bosses who leer or belittle, and nonbosses who neither praise nor put down, but also delay projects with their complete inability to make decisions, meaning that everyone has to stay until midnight the week before the deadline. Even good bosses, though, seldom have the exact same priorities you would have. The nature of the game is that the boss gets to choose the priorities. Not you. That's how Big Business works.

Like most elements of pop culture history, this tale of Big Business and the universal experience of that damn boss has never been entirely true. At the height of the Organization Man days in the 1950s, you could eat dinner at a mom-and-pop Chinese restaurant or get your auto scrubbed at the local independent car wash. Betty Friedan may have ignored them, but crafty moms have always made things like children's clothes and sold their creations, both for income and for creative self-actualization, at fairs or in local stores. Even as *The Man in the Gray Flannel Suit* hit theaters in 1956, some of those small theater operators were probably working in their blue jeans, secretly enjoying the fact that they got to watch movies for a living while everyone else was laboring in gray flannel duds.

Like Elizabeth Murray, though, these entrepreneurs faced limits on their businesses. A mom selling baby clothes had to either make her wares physically available to customers or make her catalogue and phone number available to customers so that they could call. That limited her market to people who stopped by the store, people who saw the pricey ads she took out in magazines or the Yellow Pages, or people who saw her direct mail. Since she needed a physical presence or a catalogue, she needed reasonable up-front capital to reach a big market. The surest way to get up-front capital was to have an established or wealthy relative (as Elizabeth Murray did) or to have years of experience and thus the ability to convince backers to take a chance (as the London apprenticeship system guaranteed).

Until recently, those realities made life difficult for people who avoided the rapidly consolidating world of Big Business.

As the twenty-first century starts to age a bit, Big Business has continued consolidating. North American corporate acquisitions accelerated to $839 billion in 2005, according to *CFO* magazine, up from $692 billion in 2004.

But there's been a countertrend. While conglomerates crowd one end of the spectrum, the technology of the last 10 years has created vast spaces for small businesses at the other end. The costs to start a business these days need be no more than $10 a month for a Web site. The Internet, search engines like Google, and payment mechanisms like PayPal mean that for $10 a month, any business has a potential market of the billion people on this planet who own or can find a computer.

As we talked about in the first chapter, that means that you can specialize like crazy and still make a living, without much capital or experience. In the old days, Tina Sparkles of Sparkle Craft would have needed to convince every strip mall guitar outlet owner in the country to stock her wares, or mail a glossy catalogue to everyone she thought liked music, to make sure guitar strap seekers could find her. Now, being listed toward the top on a Google search of "guitar straps" does the same thing. She can keep her collection in her basement workshop in Austin. She doesn't need thousands of dollars for advertising, or years of experience learning how to become a favored vendor for retail shops. She just has to sew cool stuff.

That means that the career universe has opened up. There are no real barriers to creating whatever job you want, throwing the product or yourself out there, and seeing which of the billion folks online wants to pony up the money for it. Out under the "long tail" of this new economy, in Chris Anderson's phrase, people will pay for all sorts of things.

Until I wrote this book, I did not know that celebrities would pay someone to create embroidered portraits of their friends' dogs. But they will. Don't assume that the thing you love, the thing you did for fun as a kid, can't be turned into a viable business.

After all, Greg Glenn makes a living playing with sand.

I'd read about a sand-sculpture business in an early 1990s Barbara Winter book on entrepreneurship called *Making a Living without a Job*. Intrigued, I went online, searched, and found Glenn's company, Sandscapes. He and a few buddies founded the firm around the time Winter's book came out. I called and learned that it was still in business 15 years later (in the chapter on Grindhopping Guideline 3 you'll learn that the oft-quoted stat that 95 percent of start-ups fail in five years is flat out false).

Glenn grew up in Huntington Beach, California, and always loved playing in the sand. He studied to be an engineer and was working as a land surveyor when a friend suggested that he participate in a United Way sand-sculpting contest at the local beach. Unlike the standard kid practice of scraping sand together, sand sculpting involves packing the sand into compact blocks, then carving images out of the blocks, as you would with marble. Unlike a marble sculpture, though, you can carve a sand sculpture in a day or two. Pure sand sculpting uses no adhesives, making the structural design critical. That appealed to Glenn's engineering background. As soon as he started sculpting, he was hooked.

> **❝Until I wrote this book, I did not know that celebrities would pay someone to create embroidered portraits of their friends' dogs. But they will. Don't assume that the thing you love, the thing you did for fun as a kid, can't be turned into a viable business.❞**

To make a long story short, he and two friends decided that, given how people flocked to snap photos of their sculptures, companies or event planners would probably pay them to create sculptures and thus draw the public to their events. For the past 15 years, Sandscapes' employees have been doing just that. They build about 50 sculptures a year, everywhere from malls to beaches. They've worked for Disney and for state fairs, and they did one particularly surreal set of sand sculptures for a design exposition in Japan that re-created scenes from Japanese fairy tales (which put the Brothers Grimm to shame in terms of violence). Glenn even met his wife while building a sand sculpture at a mall. She was working in a store, but she quit her job and came to work for him.

Glenn is still tickled about the whole enterprise. When people ask him about his job, he can honestly say that he gets paid to build stuff with sand. "This was as much a surprise to me as anyone else," he says. "We're still shocked."

I'm shocked, too, because when I went back to Winter's book, I realized that I'd found the wrong guy. Winter profiled not Glenn or one of his two cofounders, but an ex-architect who founded a company called Sand Sculptors International. Yes, the modern economy can support at least two small businesses devoted to sand sculpting.

Chances are someone will pay for one of your ideas, too. The question is how to make that happen, not whether it will.

MAKING THE CASH REGISTER RING

So once you've conjured up what you loved to do as a kid, spend some time meditating on the subject. Read about it. Mull it over while you're cooking dinner. Take a different route to somewhere you usually go to trigger different pathways in your brain. And then picture your ideal working situation. Ask, as Glenn did:

⋯⋗ **Who needs or wants what I love to do and do well?**

⋯⋗ **Why do they need it?**

In Glenn's case, he loved to build sand sculptures, and event planners needed big, gawk-worthy things that would draw people to their happenings. Once you have those answers, ask the most critical question:

⋯⋗ **What's a low-cost way I could start offering it to them and get paid quickly?**

Unless you're independently wealthy, you won't have a lot of money for start-up or operational capital. Your idea, in the words of Internet entrepreneur Brandon Guttman, "needs to be cheap, and it needs to start ringing the cash register right away." Guttman started a Web marketing company called Market Precision in 2001. You'll recall that as being a bad year for the dot-com industry. Guttman's business has survived because its revenue model wasn't tied to attracting eyeballs, then hoping that money would follow like weeds after rain. Customers paid from the start.

This is the difference between a business that's Grindhopper-friendly and one that isn't. Say you've identified your childhood love as baking sweets. This was true for Sibby Thomsen, a San Francisco resident who grew up in Topeka, Kansas, eating Nutty Bars and ice cream cones for lunch every day. She liked to bake with her mother on weekends, and she had a particular fondness for cupcakes. As a grown-up, whenever she visited a new town, she'd check out the bakery. She pursued an advertising career for several years, but then decided she needed to satisfy her professional sweet tooth. She wanted to retain creative control, which meant she couldn't build a career in someone else's confection company. So how could she turn her love of baking cupcakes into a career?

We could brainstorm several ways. Perhaps she could invent a stunning new oven that would use some mysterious force similar to microwaving that would heat cupcakes faster than a microwave, yet still brown them. More realistically, she could open a walk-in bakery that sold all sorts of pies, cakes, and confections. Or she could open a walk-in bakery that sold just cupcakes. Or she could just bake cupcakes and cater parties and events for people who want to celebrate their inner child, particularly the selfish part of their inner child that likes not having to share a cake with other people.

She wound up going with the latter. She opened Sibby's Cupcakery, a baking and catering business, in 2004. She tested recipes in her own oven at first, then rented space as needed in a commercial kitchen when she began cooking for other people, rather than building a kitchen herself. "I wanted to keep it simple," she says. Then she happened upon the perfect promotional opportunity. A friend mentioned that she was organizing a bazaar for local designers. Thomsen came up with a business name and promotional flyers, and handed out 400 cupcakes at the event. Starting a walk-in store would have meant shelling out thousands of dollars for a lease, and wages for folks to staff the place before anyone bought a cupcake. Baking 400 cupcakes in rented space, on the other hand, required an up-front investment of a pantry's worth of sugar, flour, butter, and eggs, and just a bit of cash. Word of mouth—and bazaar attendees with frosting on their lips—had Thomsen's cash register ringing and paying back that investment in no time.

Of course, starting a low-capital business doesn't mean you have to stay small. After a while, Thomsen's cash register was ringing so quickly that her rented oven couldn't handle the orders. With her proven revenue stream, she borrowed money, closed up shop for eight months, then designed and built her own commercial kitchen.

She relaunched in December 2005, and spends her days baking and, yes, eating her inventory. "I don't ever get tired of the cupcakes," she says.

GETTING BOSSY

All this talk of being your own boss as you build sand castles and bake cupcakes is fun. But plenty of people have ideas, and plenty of people would like to tell their bosses to shove off because they're going to be their own boss from now on. Few people do it.

> **To build a career without paying your dues, you have to realize that 'always be your own boss' has a corollary.**
>
> **You actually have to *be the boss of yourself*, too.**

Why? It comes down to the labor force split again. I work from home. When I mention that, I'm amazed at how many smart, professional, ambitious people respond, "Oh, I could never do that. I'd watch too much TV."

To build a career without paying your dues, you have to realize that "always be your own boss" has a corollary.

You actually have to *be the boss of yourself, too.*

Grindhoppers never want to be in a position where they have to compromise their independence, or endure a life they don't want, because they need the money or can't make things happen on their own.

So they develop phenomenal self-discipline. They practice this discipline in four key areas:

> 1 They don't care too much about external rewards.
> 2 They work hard, even if no one notices.
> 3 They don't rely on any one revenue stream.
> 4 They are frugal to a fault.

The first point is tricky. As any teacher or manager knows, external rewards are a great way to motivate people. Kids work harder in classes with tough grading systems. Salespeople who are promised a trip to Hawaii for reaching a sales target are quite likely to aim for it. Raises and promotions are external rewards, as are more vacation days, bigger offices, even motivational plaques.

Anyone who works for a boss works for external rewards. Most people are okay with that, and don't think about it too much. Then there's another school of thought, best expressed by education writer Alfie Kohn in *Punished by Rewards: The Trouble with Gold Stars, Incentive Plans, A's, Praise, and Other Bribes*. This philosophy maintains that grades and Hawaii vacation bonuses are the human equivalent of dangling a carrot in front of a hamster on his wheel. We aren't animals; bribes treat us as if we are. Kohn suggests that perhaps workers would be more productive and loyal if they were rewarded with things like autonomy, meaningful work, and the opportunity to labor together as a team to achieve something bigger than themselves.

The truth is somewhere in between. Autonomy is great, but so is cash. No one in her right mind would take a real job at someone else's company if she might not get paid for a year, would then get a paycheck only if business was swift, and would receive no feedback on her great ideas until they were completely implemented, no matter how much autonomy and meaningfulness she experienced. Yet Grindhoppers make that bargain all the time.

People, it turns out, are motivated by a combination of things. There are external rewards of the sort that most of us recognize (paychecks, gold stars) and the natural rewards that Kohn favors (autonomy, meaningfulness, watching an idea grow to fruition). When you're in the mindset of working for someone else, you figure that someone else is getting a lot of the autonomy, meaningfulness, and idea-to-fruition benefits. So your rewards had better be stacked in the external category. Otherwise, you won't work. This is true even of people who are generally hard workers. Several top business schools, for instance, don't report grades to recruiters. In essence, that means that grades don't matter. As a result, some professors at these schools have resorted to taking attendance in classes, as if their MBA students were children. The love of knowledge alone is not a sufficient incentive to get to class.

When you work for yourself, on the other hand, the autonomy and meaningfulness rewards accrue to you. So external recognition becomes less important.

In theory. In reality, all of us grew up working for good grades and gold stars. Grindhoppers got more than most. That habit means that learning to be motivated solely by natural rewards is frighteningly difficult.

It's also necessary if you want to be your own boss. Yes, Grindhoppers often achieve external rewards such as money or praise. But these are never givens. There's no boss to guarantee you'll get them. You can try to approximate them. Talk to a Grindhopper for a while and she'll admit to adding up her anticipated income or printing laudatory e-mails because she wants that gold star. I suspect that some of the Grindhoppers who agreed to speak with me for this book did so because they wanted external validation that they were successful. Learning not to care about such kudos takes incredible discipline. The more confident Grindhoppers do it. The rest of us just keep trying.

The second way Grindhoppers practice self-discipline is by working hard, even if it would be easier not to. Note that I said working hard, not working long. There's a difference.

Our culture makes a fetish of overwork, particularly among young people. The 2006 *Statistical Abstract of the United States* says that about 28 percent of us work more than 40 hours a week (8 percent work more than 60), but I've spent enough time around urban 20- and 30-something professionals to know that 10- to 12-hour days are pretty much the norm in these spheres.

Nancy Collins experienced this reality firsthand. I first interviewed this Chicago-area Grindhopper in 2002 for a *USA Today* column I wrote called "White-Collar Sweatshops Batter Young Workers." Collins had spent a few years in her early twenties working for JP Morgan, the investment bank. She told me about toiling for a boss that colleagues nicknamed "The Prince of Darkness" for his tendency to make people work until 2 a.m. She told me about being assigned to two projects at once during a stint in Australia. She came home from work one morning at 7 a.m. after weeks of 18-hour days and constant travel. Not to sleep. To shower. As she stood there in the water, she began to cry. "I started thinking, there's got to be more to life than this," she told me.

JP Morgan—as I learned from the e-mails that arrived after that column appeared—isn't the only company that's driving its young employees insane. If you rattle off the biggest offenders, from Goldman Sachs to Boston Consulting Group, you wind up with a near approximation of the list of companies that advertise for new hires in Ivy League college newspapers. All hire the brightest parolees from college and graduate school and make them a deal. We will pay you $60,000 or more a year and give you glimpses of corporate luxury like ritzy hotel stays and business-class plane tickets. In exchange, you will work 70, 80, even 100 hours a week through the best years of your life.

That's fine if you want to take that deal. What gets me is when people claim that working 80 hours a week is evidence that someone has a good work ethic. Let's not pretend that such long hours are necessarily good hours, defined as hours that efficiently advance you toward the life you want. When I worked at *Fortune* for a summer in college, the magazine would buy you dinner if you stayed after 8 p.m., and would pay a driver to take you home if you stayed until 9 p.m. Since reporters at the time earned an hourly wage with time-and-a-half for overtime, if you didn't have anything else going on any particular night, the temptation to be less efficient was strong. Likewise, lawyers work long hours in part to achieve the number of billable hours their firms require, not necessarily because each client needed every single hour billed. If your consulting team engages in a three-hour conference call that results in only 20 minutes of work getting done, you're not working hard. Indeed, you're hardly working at all.

Let's also not pretend that white-collar sweatshop hours are evidence that evil companies are exploiting people. Listen to young bankers talk about their work and you can hear the pride under the complaining. You worked 80 hours this week? Well, I worked 90. You slept four hours? Well, I slept at the office and showered there, too. In college, our generation vied for status by comparing work-loads. After school, the conversations didn't change. A high-wattage job fills an almost religious need to be part of something bigger than yourself, and working 14-hour days means that you don't have to deal with the messiness of life.

Grindhoppers, on the other hand, hate inefficiencies. One of the reasons they hop out of the grind is the grind's emphasis on busy-ness, as opposed to achieving results. Sometimes they work long. But they definitely work hard. They are persistent. They don't allow themselves any excuses for failure.

Collins didn't. After leaving JP Morgan and earning an MBA from Harvard, she started an adventure travel agency called Global Adrenaline shortly before September 11, 2001. Despite her stellar business credentials, this was an atrocious time to start an international travel business. For a while, every time the phone rang, she would leap to answer it, only to discover that it was a telemarketer. She couldn't pay herself for the first few years the company existed.

But she kept at it, leading and selling tours to Africa, Asia, and the Arctic. She still works weekends. That's Collins's personality, and that's part of building a business. But now, "When I wake up Sunday morning and go to work, that's my choice," she says. "I value that a lot." The day we spoke on the phone, she walked out of the office before 5 p.m. (though she worked a bit after dinner to stay on top of things).

The third way Grindhoppers exercise self-discipline is by making sure that they don't become too reliant on any one revenue stream. They juggle projects, not jobs, so that if one becomes intolerable or threatens to disappear, they don't need to compromise their independence to keep or replace it. This takes effort. It's easier to assume that your current gig or gigs will always be there, but as folks forced to read *Who Moved My Cheese?* before corporate restructurings have learned, that might not be the case. There's more on this in Grindhopping Guideline 4, "Think Projects, Not Jobs."

BUYING YOUR TICKET OUT

Developing your own reward structure, working hard, and creating backup plans will take you far toward building your dream career. But ultimately, you won't be able to build that rewarding career if you have to work 60 hours a week for someone else just to cover your lifestyle costs. That's why the most important place Grindhoppers need self-discipline is in their pocketbooks.

> **The old saying is incomplete. Money doesn't buy you love or happiness. It buys you freedom. Six months of expenses in the bank is your ticket to life outside the grind.**

The old saying is incomplete. Money doesn't buy you love or happiness. It buys you freedom. Six months of expenses in the bank is your ticket to life outside the grind.

I can't emphasize this enough. People get stuck in jobs they don't like because they become addicted to seeing a pot of money appear in their checking accounts every two weeks. More than half of Americans (52 percent) live paycheck to paycheck, according to a 2003 MetLife Employee Benefits Survey. That includes 59 percent of those aged 21 to 30. Even well-to-do people rely on that cash infusion. A third (34 percent) of those earning more than $75,000 a year lives paycheck to paycheck. As a chemist with an interest in personal finance once told me, people are like gases. Our "needs" expand to fill the space our incomes create. When we're poor, we season our meat with salt or barbecue sauce. When we're rich, we need that Williams-Sonoma grilling paste. According to the Bureau of Economic Analysis, the average personal savings rate was actually –0.5 percent (that's a minus sign) during the first two months of 2006.

One of the reasons this rate has fallen from 8 to 10 percent in the 1970s is the widespread availability of consumer credit. When our parents bought our baby clothes, they probably couldn't charge those too-cute pajamas unless they bought them at a department store with its own charge card. Now, our world of low-introductory-rate offers and mysteriously glamorous TV apartments says that you can have whatever you want, now. That's why the Federal Reserve calculates revolving consumer debt—usually involving credit cards—at $800 billion, or approximately $8,000 per household. Young adults are particularly susceptible to this message. As with obesity statistics, I'm inclined to believe just about any horrible number I read about young Americans' debt problems. I clip articles with leads like this one, from an M.P. Dunleavey column on MSN Money:

Lyndsey graduated from college in 2000 with no debt whatsoever. But a funny thing happened on the way to adulthood. Despite an enviable salary of $43,000 a year and paying only $600 a month in rent for the Arlington, Va., house she shares with three roommates, she's now $12,000 in the hole and not quite sure how she got there.

I'm not sure, either. But I can guess. Demos, a progressive think tank, tried to lobby against the recent bankruptcy reform law by publishing a study in 2004 called "Generation Broke." The study claimed that current economic realities make the path to adulthood more perilous for today's young adults than what baby boomers experienced. Average student loan debt rose from about $9,000 in 1992 to $18,900 in 2002 (not Lyndsey's problem, but a fact nonetheless). Real wages climbed only 5 to 7 percent (again, with a solid $43,000 for an entry-level job, not Lyndsey's problem—but a fact).

To prove that these numbers don't add up, Demos presented the average budget, based on consumer surveys, for a 2001 graduate—

we'll call him "Grad"—earning the average new hire salary of $36,000. On Grad's take-home pay of $2,058 a month, after paying for rent and utilities in an urban market ($797); car payments, gas, and auto insurance ($464); food ($456); student loans ($182); and credit card minimums ($125), he has $34 left. Total.

If he saves that for three months, he can buy a bus ticket to Mom's house to sleep under his old *Star Wars* comforter. If he tries to make it on his own, we can see how he might wind up $12,000 in the hole.

Closer inspection, though, finds that Grad's average budget is less structurally sound than a sand sculpture. How do I know? I graduated in 2001. My first job paid a lot less than Grad's miserly $36,000 salary. So I put myself on the austerity plan. I shared a house with three girls. I couldn't afford a car, so I took the bus to work and bummed rides from my boss. I clipped coupons and bought generic groceries. I cooked casseroles on the weekends so I could brown-bag my lunches during the week. I bought suits at discount stores. I borrowed books from the library. Since I had only myself to look after, I lived on about $1,000 a month in a major city. As a result of this austerity plan, I saved enough to travel to Asia for a few weeks after my year-long internship ended in the summer of 2002, and to finance my move to New York after that.

I didn't feel particularly deprived. Well, maybe I did on one sad Saturday when I found myself boiling chicken bones to make soup stock. As I stood there skimming fat from the pot, I decided that I could justify spending 99 cents a can for the generic stuff. But mostly, I discovered that living with roommates meant that even a boring weekday night was a small party. My cooking evolved over the year to become a lot better than the office cafeteria food. Riding the bus to work gave me the chance to read *Anna Karenina*.

Quite simply, I didn't want to go into debt. I wanted money in the bank. That money would save me from taking jobs I didn't want in the future just because I needed cash. That was my priority. Living true to your priorities isn't deprivation. It's a choice—to say no to impulses and yes to things you want more.

Yet somehow the Demos figures wound up appearing in various articles as evidence that young people are doomed.

Whatever. Society hasn't lost its ladder to financial stability. Young people have lost interest in starting out poor. Their massive credit card debts are the inevitable result. Live within your means, though, and you'll achieve the kind of financial independence that lets you build a career without becoming trapped in a real, dues-paying job.

Financial planners differ on how much cash you need in the bank to avoid that trap. The average length of unemployment is four to five months, so that's why many say to plan for six months. If you, as a young, ambitious graduate, truly want to be employed, it will not take you five months to find *something*. But that same little nest egg *will* give you time to try your grind-free career idea. If it doesn't pan out, you can always find a part-time gig after three months or so. After another month or two, if your idea still isn't working, you can hunt for a full-time job in earnest. But a six-month cushion at least gives you the chance to try the life you want.

Here's how you build up your bank account. First, figure out what you absolutely need to live on. Make a list of all your expenses by month, prorating any quarterly or annual payments. Then figure out how you'd trim this list if you had little or no money coming in. Get a dollar number. Be honest. In most cities, even if you have student loan payments, the austerity burn rate need not be more than $1,500 a month for an individual (you didn't buy yourself a new car as a graduation present, did you?). In New York, when I had to pay for an HMO instead of the cheap catastrophic insurance I had been carrying, my burn rate jumped to $1,800 a month, but I could have lived in a cheaper apartment. Add 10 percent to this number for walking-around money if you wish, and you'll feel rich.

Save everything else that comes in. Multiply your austerity number by 6 to get a savings target. For instance, $1,500 times six months is $9,000.

If you don't have credit card debt and you live and eat cheaply, you can reach that target and start building your dream career after about 18 months at Grad's salary. At Lyndsey's pay, especially if you don't have loans, you could be free after nine months. If you've managed to accrue some savings during college, you might be able to hop out of the grind six months after you graduate, or even sooner if you keep a part-time job while you build your Grindhopping career.

If you have serious loans, you may need to keep moonlighting for a bit if your ventures don't make the cash register ring as quickly as you'd like. That's fine. Student loans are an investment. But financial self-discipline means not going into debt for anything that's not an investment. If charging something means you won't be able to pay your credit card bill in full, don't buy it. Even if it's groceries. I don't buy the line from the various Generational Spokespeople that says that young people are indebted because they're charging necessities. You can eat for a day on what people pay for their morning venti cappuccino at Starbucks.

GETTING IN THE HABIT

I know that making tasty dinners out of Ramen noodles can be tough, even if you do spice up the recipe with celery and spinach. Self-discipline is tough. You can't pop on the tube all the time if you're working from home. If you're starting a small business, you need to hold yourself to everything on your to-do list, even if no one is watching you. You need to dream up your to-do list without anyone insisting that you do anything but stay in bed and drink (cheap) Chianti all day.

For all these reasons, some people think self-discipline is *too* tough. Like anything, though, it can be learned. All it boils down to is getting into the habit of keeping promises to yourself.

You allow yourself no excuses for failure. A boss wouldn't allow excuses, and now you're the boss. You hold yourself accountable to these promises, day by day.

If you're trying to cultivate the habit of discipline, you can tone your muscles in this area by choosing two promises to keep.

> **For all these reasons, some people think self-discipline is *too* tough. Like anything, though, it can be learned. All it boils down to is getting into the habit of keeping promises to yourself.**

The first should be an exercise goal that's beyond what you do now. Commit to keep the promise for at least 30 days. One Grindhopper told me that he vowed to run 30 days in a row when he turned 30. He didn't feel like it some days, but he did it anyway. Then he decided he liked it. When I interviewed him for this book, he was training for a marathon. Whatever your physical goal, be sure to record it. Do not let yourself break the promise unless you're ill and physically unable to move. Don't "reward" yourself for keeping your promise, either. Self-discipline is breaking the habit of expecting a treat every time you fetch

42

the paper. The natural rewards of doing something physical will show next time you put on a bathing suit.

Then choose another habit. Maybe you'll pledge to thank God or whatever power you believe in daily for your blessings. Not a bad idea. Professor Robert Emmons at the University of California–Davis has made a career of studying gratitude. People who are grateful, he's discovered, have better health, have more energy, and are more likely to make progress toward big goals than those who don't count their blessings. Maybe you'll promise to write in a journal every day. Or you'll pledge to read Greek for 30 minutes. Whatever your habit, record it. Do not let yourself break the promise. If you have to scribble Greek on a sheet of paper because you forgot your book and are traveling, do it.

It takes a few weeks for habits to gel, so keep up the experiment with each of these promises for at least a month or two. You'll probably be so happy with the results that you'll continue. You'll teach yourself not to quit just because quitting is easier and there's no boss saying that you can't. You're your own boss now. And you're the most demanding boss—but the best—you'll ever have.

GRINDHOPPING
GUIDELINE #2:

KNOW WHERE *YOU'RE* GOING
It's the only way to drive on unmarked roads

"Fortune favors the prepared mind."
—Louis Pasteur (1822–1895)

W
hen you graduate from college, people line up to shake your hand and wish you luck. There's nothing wrong with that. You'll need a lot of luck if you want to build a rewarding career without paying your dues. You'll need big breaks and big opportunities. Problems arise, though, when you start viewing these things as the province of fairy godmothers who swoop down and grant your every wish. Spend a few years in the real world, and you'll be amazed at how many people deal with life in this passive way. They think, oh, I'd like to be rich at some point. I'd like to be on TV. Wouldn't that be fun? There are people who dream of traveling around the world who don't have valid passports. A fairy godmother encountering that situation not only has to arrange the trip, she has to stand in line at the post office with two mug shots of you. Chances are, she won't bother.

Successful Grindhoppers know that fairy godmothers are lazy people.

They also know that luck is not a matter of chance.

Indeed, Richard Wiseman, a British psychologist who studies the phenomenon of luck, notes in his book *The Luck Factor* that lucky people actually create their own good fortune through four actions and personality traits. First, they look relentlessly on the bright side. An unlucky person who is shot in the arm during a bank robbery will moan about being in the wrong place. A lucky person will say, "I could have been shot in the head!" Second, lucky people expect good fortune. They wake up in the morning wondering what wonderful thing will happen to them that day. Something wonderful usually does. Third, lucky people trust themselves and listen to their hunches. They boost their intuitive abilities by meditating and clearing their minds of distracting thoughts. Finally, lucky people have a knack for creating, noticing, and acting on chance opportunities.

It is this last skill that will best help you build a career outside the grind.

Grindhoppers figure out where they need to be for fortune to spot them. Then they figure out how they will get to that place. In other words, they set big goals, Goals with a capital G. Then they set smaller goals that help them reach the big ones.

Most of the Grindhoppers I interviewed for this book told me that they planned their careers this way. They knew starting out that they couldn't follow a set path that junior account managers before them had blazed to the senior account manager level. So they had to dream up the plans for their lives, although many of the more free-spirited ones winced when I mentioned the "G word." They preferred to come across like Walt Whitman musing on "Spontaneous Me." After all, a five-year plan and a goal-setting strategy sound dangerously corporate. So these Grindhoppers gave me various deep-sounding statements like, "Life's a journey, not a destination," or, "The path is formed by walking on it."

> **Grindhoppers figure out where they need to be for fortune to spot them. Then they figure out how they will get to that place. In other words, they set big goals, Goals with a capital G. Then they set smaller goals that help them reach the big ones.**

Don't be fooled. Grindhoppers may be forming their paths by clearing brush through the desert and enjoying the journey as they do so, but they can see the mountains peeking over the horizon. They know where they're going. They think about the future constantly. They know that eventually the days of "when I grow up" will be upon them, and when that happens, their dreams will no longer be able to inhabit the when-I-grow-up world. They know that if you want to build a career outside the grind, then eventually you must make your own luck happen, or at least get close enough to where you need to be that all your fairy godmother has to do is hit the remote control you put in her hand.

So Grindhoppers do just that. If a Grindhopper wants to write a best-selling novel, for instance, he'll research what kinds of plots sell. He'll set aside three hours a day to write so that he can crank out 2,000 words a week for the next 35 weeks or so, because he knows that first novels usually clock in at 70,000 words. He'll arrange for writers he respects to give him feedback. He'll work his network to find literary agents who are interested in handling manuscripts like his. He'll think through what the cover should look like, and how he'll market the novel to the target reading audience. He'll create a promotional plan, line up endorsements, and get buzz going about his tale. Sure, it will be a stroke of "luck" when he lands a publishing deal and when his creation starts flying off the shelves. He may even speak of it that way. But for all his talk of the universe's whimsy, in truth, he made the arrangements. His fairy godmother just gave the final tap. Or, as a Grindhopper named Brittany Blockman, who runs the film company Third Room Productions, told me, "I come across as spontaneous and whimsical to people, but I'm always thinking ahead. I have a million things I want to do, and I have a little plan for each."

The big thing that Blockman and her business partner, Josephine Decker, have wanted to do lately is produce a documentary on bisexuality called *Bi the Way*. By all appearances, their moviemaking venture has been rather spontaneous and whimsical. When they started making the film, they decided to take a western road trip to score footage, following a bisexual Brooklyn woman out to California with her new boyfriend, who was training to be a cage fighter. To save cash, they and their three-person crew would all cram into the same motel room most nights. They also got lost so often that "a lot of the film is shot when the sun's going down," Blockman told me. Fading light is good light, but you get only one take. At one low moment, they pulled into Socorro, New Mexico, after missing three exits. They had ten minutes of light left to interview a polyamorous woman about her girlfriend and two boyfriends.

It's a story that really deserved more time.

Of course, it's also the kind of story that Blockman and Decker have had a blast telling. Both of them had wanted to make movies from the time they were girls. They met during their freshman year at Princeton and talked about forming a production company with their friends. There's nothing surprising about that. Plenty of spontaneous and whimsical teenagers talk about making films. Being the Grindhopping sort, though, Blockman and Decker actually hatched plans for building their moviemaking careers alongside the talk. Blockman shot a documentary about an AIDS hospice for her senior thesis, which landed her a spot on the runner up list in *Glamour* magazine's Top 10 College Women contest. Decker took a job at ABC News Productions for a year after graduating. Then another production company brought her on to help create a show on spirituality for the Hallmark channel. At first, she was excited about presenting the world's great religions to viewers. Then she watched the project get watered down by folks who thought that the average viewer couldn't handle Hinduism. She grew frustrated, and she decided to join forces with Blockman to produce the kind of films that they wanted to see. Their first project? A mockumentary called *Naked Princeton* about a fictional Ivy League nudist society. They had so much fun shooting the film that they decided to try to push their moviemaking careers to the next level.

That's when they had a big stroke of "luck." After showing *Naked Princeton* at a small film festival, they were shopping it around to others when they got a casual meeting with Michael Huffington, former congressman, famed bisexual, and ex-husband of pundit Arianna. In addition to his political jobs, Huffington had spent some time running a documentary company. Blockman and Decker told him about their moviemaking experiences. He told them he was thinking of getting back into film production. They pounced. They pitched *Bi the Way*. Third Room Productions' fairy godmother waved her wand, and Huffington agreed to produce the piece. Our moviemaking heroines took off running.

Of course, it's not exactly an accident that these two young women walked into a meeting with a known bisexual film financer with a proposal for a movie that they knew would be close to his heart. Blockman got the inspiration for *Bi the Way* by watching an episode of *The O.C.* that featured bisexual characters. She was struck by how open today's teen shows were about such things, and she thought that the more flexible sexualities of today's young people would make good film fodder. But she and Decker had been kicking around other ideas, too. If they'd gotten a meeting with a patron who said she wanted to produce a movie on health issues, that person might have been pitched a version of Blockman's hospice thesis. A financer with an interest in international issues might have been pitched a movie on orphanages. Lucky people, Richard Wiseman notes, have an ability to create, notice, and act on chance opportunities. Blockman and Decker walked into the Huffington meeting prepared to act on any opening that was made available. With that mindset, getting a big break was just a matter of time.

It's a mindset that they've continued employing as they've been producing *Bi the Way*. They wanted to create a colorful, compelling movie. To do that, they knew they needed as much colorful, compelling footage as possible. So they put themselves in situations that were likely to create such shots—showing up at Brigham Young University in Utah, for instance, and asking folks if there were any bisexuals on campus. As they got kicked out of this Mormon enclave, they let the cameras roll.

It will also be a great stroke of "luck" when they get *Bi the Way* aired on a major network. But to give their lazy fairy godmother a nudge, they've produced a trailer and met with Al Gore's Current TV network and with MTV, and they are trying to meet with HBO. They also try to spend a few hours every weekend writing a script to turn *Naked Princeton* into a feature-length film, so that they'll have something in the pipeline to capitalize on any future *Bi the Way* buzz.

In other words, Blockman and Decker know where they are going. Even if they got lost on the way to Socorro, New Mexico, and had to sleep five to a room, there has been nothing spontaneous or whimsical about the way they've been building their film careers. Breaking big goals into manageable chunks of your own choosing is the way dreams become reality. *Any* dream. If you want to be a millionaire when you retire, you can hope to win the lottery. Or you can make your own luck by socking away $5,000 a year in index funds for the next 40 years. Then you'd have to be pretty *unlucky* not to retire with seven figures to your name.

CHARTING A PATH

Figuring out where we're going and how we're going to get there is critical to success outside the grind. Unfortunately, few of us learn to deal with life this way when we're growing up. In school, eighth grade followed seventh grade like day follows night. If you finished 13 years of primary and secondary schooling, you earned a high school diploma. Applying to college might have introduced an element of uncertainty, but once you were there, earning that philosophy degree involved taking and passing a certain sequence of courses. You moved forward by showing up. The corporate world is changing from this philosophy, but slowly. A June 2005 survey from the Hudson Highland Group found that 60 percent of workers believe that tenure, not performance, determines pay where they work.

Breaking free from such structures to build your own career and make your own luck is like scaling a cliff when you've always been climbing ladders. It isn't easy. Some people postpone the climb by staying in school long past the point of diminishing returns. Others stumble into an angst-ridden state that's been chronicled by a whole shelf of books with names like *Quarterlife Crisis* or *Midlife Crisis at 30*.

But such crises are not inevitable. Like self-discipline, "knowing where you're going" is a skill that can be learned.

Most Grindhoppers aren't starting from zero in this regard at graduation. Because they find their chosen work fascinating, they've landed internships in their fields during the summers. They've done volunteer work or are working part-time in these areas during the school year to keep their skills and contacts current. They read about their fields constantly.

But even if you are starting from near the ground, you can still figure out where you're going and how you're going to get there. First, you need to spend some serious time thinking about your ideal career and your ideal life—the things we talked about in Grindhopping Guideline 1. Think about what you want your career and your life to look like. Be bold. Be crazy. But don't skip this step. It's tough to get where you're going if you don't let yourself imagine where that place might be.

Once you've got an image, then you can start to turn your dream life into reality. You do that by getting a notebook, getting on Google, talking with everyone you know, and hunting for all relevant information on how you will break your big goals into doable chunks. Then you make a plan to do just that.

When Grindhopper Syl Tang launched the digital HipGuide— listings of cool restaurants, stores, and parties in nine cities from

Paris to Miami—she knew she needed to market herself as a guru of all things hip. So she studied how other arbiters of taste had built their brands. In particular, she studied Martha Stewart. She made a timeline of Stewart's career, from catering to cookbooks to magazines to TV host. Then she tried to figure out which elements she could pull off. Tang's articles on style for the *Financial Times* and her media appearances are based, in part, on the lessons she learned from Stewart's timeline.

Tang realized that while her path was unconventional, she didn't have to invent it completely from scratch. Neither do you. If you want to build a career outside the grind, study the bios of people who've done big things in the same industry. For instance, if you want to make documentary films, you might read magazine and newspaper stories about Morgan Spurlock or Aviva Slesin. You could go to different film schools' Web pages and see what subjects, films, and texts these institutions have their students absorb. Whatever your dream career, go to Borders and spend a few evenings taking notes from books in the stacks (not from this book—you should purchase this book). Flip through trade magazines and visit industry Web sites. Read blogs from other folks in the field to see what the big obstacles and controversies might be. Learn the language and read FAQs so that you don't ask dumb questions that show you haven't done your homework ("Wow, magazine writers get paid by the word? So aren't you tempted to put a lot of extra words in there so that you get paid more?").

Next, interview three people who have pursued similar career paths. If you're starting a business designing hip embroidery patterns, maybe you won't be able to find someone who's doing the exact same thing. But you might be able to find a woman who designs knitting patterns for her popular learn-to-knit seminars. Or you might find someone who sells ethnic scrapbooking stickers and other supplies online. Make sure you choose people in slightly different stages of their careers. Ask them how they got where they are. If you've done your homework first, they'll probably be thrilled to talk. It's flattering to be asked for advice. It's even more flattering if the person doesn't want anything from you beyond information. So don't ask for projects or jobs at your first meeting.

Armed with this information, picture the elements you'd like to have in your dream career, and write down the steps you need to take to get there. Then you can figure out what's a reasonable time frame for all these actions. A year? Ten years? What can you do in the next month? The next week? Tomorrow? If there is something you can do tomorrow or in the next week, be sure to find space for it on your to-do list. Building your ideal life and career is certainly as high a priority as anything else you've got wedged in there.

Plenty of Grindhoppers do set goals in exactly this fashion. My friend Christine, a writer, uses a program called Stickies to put electronic Post-It notes on her computer screen, where she's forced to look at them as she works. These Stickies tell her what she should be doing to crank out copy and build a platform for her next book during any given day, week, month, or whenever.

Justin "Red" Sanders, a video production entrepreneur in Fort Worth, Texas, is also big on specific goals. When I spoke with him recently, he peppered his Texas speech with the dreaded G word so many times that I lost count. Since he had ten years of experience in audio and video productions by age 23, though, I wasn't surprised to learn that he knew where he was going and had plans to get there.

As a kid, Sanders used to wander into the local Radio Shack to stare at the sound mixing equipment. He didn't know what all the buttons did, but he did know he wanted to try them. He saved up money from mowing lawns to buy a machine, then volunteered to DJ a local school luncheon. He charmed the attendees so much that he left with $800 worth of future business from that first booking. Indeed, the referrals poured in at such a rate that he hired an older man who'd worked in radio to assist him. Most people at the events—weddings, parties, and so on—assumed that Sanders was working for the other man. No matter. An older face made people comfortable and kept the gigs coming.

By his freshman year in high school, Sanders noticed that while video recordings of events were becoming popular, no other DJs in his area were offering a video option as part of their services. He got his hands on a video camera and started toting that along to weddings. He loved exploring angles and mixing in music with the scenes. To learn more about this new interest, he did an internship at a Dallas video production company called ReelFX. It was a small venture, but one with big clients, such as Coca-Cola. All summer he absorbed how the ReelFX folks made their videos and dealt with customers. He decided that he, too, could build a company that would do this.

He went to Texas Christian University to study film. While there, he convinced Coca-Cola to let him produce a video for executives that touted a new sales incentive program. TCU hired him to film a national TV commercial for the school that aired during football games on ESPN and Fox Sports. He worked for a local megachurch that wanted to entice worshippers with MTV-style video during services.

At some point during all this, he set a goal of going into the music video production business. Being the Grindhopping sort, he dreamed up a plan while he dreamed up that goal. He decided to produce videos for five up-and-coming bands and hope one of the bands hit it big. He went to London for a term abroad and decided that the Water Rats Theatre would be a good venue to scout for such bands. He pulled up the schedule, saw an interesting looking band called Keane, listened to a sound clip, and decided to check it out. Before long, other people were checking it out, too. The band signed with a major label, toured with U2—and used a lot of Sanders's footage in its own documentary video.

Now that he's out of school, Sanders has become more serious about setting goals that will put him on the path from being a small video production company to being a bigger one. He told me he'd set a goal in 2005 to double his 2004 revenue. He hit it by Thanksgiving. He figures out what kinds of clients he'd like to work for and then figures out how he'll lure them in. He sets goals for how big his company will be and goals for having a bigger social impact (such as producing a training video for a mission group).

All these goals and plans have kept Sanders from experiencing the quarterlife crisis he saw many of his friends struggle with. "I remember one day in the shower it hit me," he says. "I realized that when I graduated, I never gave a second thought to what I'd do." If you know where you're going (or do the hard work of self-reflection necessary to figure it out), you can skip a lot of angst along the way. Then, all your friends will think you're lucky. You are. But only because of luck that you made yourself.

TAKING THE SCENIC ROUTE

Admittedly, Sanders was blessed to figure out his calling so young. Many of us are similarly blessed, but then we ignore the calling because it sounds like a lot of work. Or we misinterpret it. We like helping people, so we think we should be doctors because that's the most obvious, prestigious route. Sometimes we become too rigid. Sanders could have stuck to his original DJ business model and ignored the rise of portable video equipment if he hadn't realized it was the production and music parts of his job that he liked, not just the parties.

That's why "knowing where you're going" requires flexibility and a lot of self-reflection. Goals need not be tattooed on your thigh.

If you meet a dashing stranger who wants to whisk you to Paris in June, and your June goal was to organize your desk, well, raid Office Depot next month. Most likely, one of your biggest goals is to have an exciting life. The sojourn in Paris will keep you on the right path for that. Part of the joy of working for yourself—coupled with the financial stability that self-discipline creates—is the ability to do something crazy just because you want to.

> **"Knowing where you're going" requires flexibility and a lot of self-reflection. Goals need not be tattooed on your thigh.**

Smart Grindhoppers realize this. So they rank their goals based on what's most important for living the lives they want. Then they learn to be flexible with specific smaller goals (which network will air *Bi The Way*), while keeping the bigger ones firm (reaching a wide audience and producing a respected film).

Grindhopper Guillermo Trias, for instance, had a big goal of acclimating American taste buds to Spanish food. While tapas-style meals are gaining favor on the East Coast, you rarely see an aisle in a Kroger or A&P devoted to Spanish food the way you see aisles of spaghetti sauce. Born in Madrid, Trias saw no reason that Americans in the heartland couldn't have the same familiarity with Spanish cuisine as they do with Italian.

His original idea was to form a consulting company that would help Spanish food manufacturers market their products in the Midwest. He knew that would be a low-capital (read: Grindhopper-friendly) way to enter the business. He started Solex Partners during his last year at Northwestern University's Kellogg School of Management, traveled to Spain, and met with a large ham producer to propose ways for the company to boost market share.

He landed the project. He did raise sales some—but then he hit a solid wall on growth capacity that resembled a block of Manchego cheese. No one was on the ground educating Midwestern grocery store owners about Spanish foods, he learned. Even if grocers did want Spanish foods, no American company was importing them for the Midwestern market. No distribution system targeted leading-edge stores and influential customers. He could not place his client's products anywhere but specialized food boutiques under the existing system.

Trias never changed his big goal of promoting Spanish foods. But the dearth of Midwestern Spanish food distributors did lead him to change his smaller goal (starting a consulting company) to a different one (starting the Spanish food importing company that the market lacked). Rather than show manufacturers how to push Serrano ham and Manchego cheese into stores, he decided to distribute the goods himself. Suddenly, instead of sitting in meetings in suits, he was touring warehouses, raising capital to lease trucks, and making deliveries. "I was the first driver for the company," Trias says. "I have carried more ham and cheese than any other MBA in the world." When he's not in work clothes and boots, he dons aprons and gives Spanish cooking demonstrations in supermarkets, smiling at his former MBA colleagues when they stop in to pick up groceries. In another ten years, he may go back to consulting. But in the meantime, he's enjoying this slightly grittier life as an ambassador for Spanish food, introducing words like *chorizo* to Midwestern moms and reminding consumers that Spain's olives are every bit as good as Italy's.

Even if they know that their goals can be flexible, though, some Grindhoppers chafe at the idea of spelling things out at all. These "life's a journey, not a destination" free spirits do still know where they're going. But their methods of getting where they're going don't involve printing out directions from Mapquest. Instead, these Grindhoppers prefer the method of constant self-reflection. They check the horizon frequently to make sure they're still on the right path.

Before these Grindhoppers do anything, they ask, is this getting me closer to where I want to be? They know that there's a difference between taking the scenic route and getting sidetracked.

Unfortunately, unless you're staring at the map or the horizon, this can be difficult to ascertain. Sometimes things that look like shortcuts have you heading toward Santa Fe instead of Socorro.

The biggest offenders here are graduate programs and prestigious jobs. Our credential-happy society is obsessed with both. Sometimes they're good ideas. But when it comes to dream careers, both must be handled with care.

For instance, perhaps your dream job involves excavating ship-wrecks off Cuba, exploring sunken Egyptian cities, and hunting dinosaur bones wherever you can find them. Thinking that you need the proper credentials, you double major in paleontology and marine studies. Then—what a coup!—you find a PhD program that lets you pursue an interdisciplinary doctorate in these subjects. This takes you seven years. You work on a small, local project identifying squirrel fossils that have already been excavated from a salt-water flat bed because that's what your thesis advisor deems important. Of course, earning a PhD points you toward the academic route. So you take a postdoctorate position at a prestigious university doing grunt work in some big name professor's research sweatshop. You teach biology to satisfy your fellowship requirements. You'd like to teach paleontology, but, as the head of your lab points out, the academic job market isn't exactly brisk.

While you're grading bio labs, you hunt around for a tenure-track position that will allow you to do the research you really want to do. Your contract ends after two years, so you jump to an adjunct position. You keep teaching biology for the next three years as you try to put together enough research papers to convince the powers that be that you deserve some grants.

Finally, success! You win some funds, which help you snare the holy grail of academia, an assistant professorship at the University of Illinois at Chicago. Then you look around to make your name—and you realize that you're years behind Sue Hendrickson, a high school dropout who just went and did all the things that you wanted to do (including finding "Sue," the most complete Tyrannosaurus rex skeleton ever located). To add insult to injury, your university decides to give her an honorary PhD.

Fundamentally, if you want a nonconventional career, at some point you're going to have to leave the well-trodden route and start driving on unmarked roads. Grindhoppers evaluate postgraduate degrees by asking whether they'll help them drive or just postpone the inevitable.

Likewise, I cringe every time I hear someone say she's going to go earn an MFA because she wants to be a writer. Getting an MFA doesn't make you a writer. Writing makes you a writer.

Prestigious jobs can be tricky, too. Sometimes they help you make contacts. Sometimes they help you gain more experience than you would be able to create on your own. Nancy Collins, from the chapter on Grindhopping Guideline 1, would have had a steeper learning curve starting her travel agency if she hadn't punched the clock at JP Morgan for a few years out of college. Young people who work at consulting firms such as McKinsey for two years can meet people from half a dozen companies during their tenure. Sometimes prestigious jobs pay a lot (enough to pay off your student loans years ahead of time), and sometimes they show future employers or clients that you're the real deal.

> **Fundamentally, if you want a nonconventional career, at some point you're going to have to leave the well-trodden route and start driving on unmarked roads. Grindhoppers evaluate postgraduate degrees by asking whether they'll help them drive or just postpone the inevitable.**

But sometimes "good" jobs put you back on the Santa Fe road when you meant to take the Socorro exit.

Photographer Catherine Hall faced that temptation recently. She knew there was nothing in jetting around the world that was antithetical to her goal of making a living off her pictures. Indeed, she sold her exotic photos of Buddhist monks and Peruvian children to publications such as *National Geographic Traveler*. The question of whether to take a full-time job on the business side of photography, however, was not such a clear call.

Hall had done a few freelance projects for Getty Images, a prestigious photo agency, to earn some cash. A full-time position scheduling photo shoots and other such things opened up. She would have been working with the biggest-name photographers in the business. The pay was decent and steady. Everyone was telling her that this was the right path to pursue. Indeed, right about the time she was mulling over taking the job, an editor that she respected savaged her photo portfolio. Maybe, she thought, she didn't have the talent to make it in this cutthroat field. "I almost said screw it," she says. "I want insurance and paid vacation and all those things."

But then she remembered that she wanted to be Catherine Hall, photographer, not Catherine Hall, scheduler. A full-time position would not have left her the time or mental energy she needed to pursue her goal of taking even better photos, the kind that editors she respected wouldn't tear apart. She knew she needed to create such a portfolio if she wanted the fairy godmother of the photography business to grant her a big break. So she didn't go for the job.

When I asked Hall how she could be so sure of herself, she told me about another low moment. She had been traveling in India during the terrorist attacks of September 11, 2001. Everyone she knew and loved was in the United States, but all flights into the country were grounded. India is a challenging place for a foreigner at the best of times; images of America being attacked made her frightfully homesick. And she couldn't get home.

So she sat on her hotel roof deck in Varanasi, in the thick Indian heat, and took stock of her life. She realized that if everything ended right then, "I thought, I wouldn't change one step that I've made in my life. I wouldn't do one thing different. I would want to be exactly where I am now." And that thought, as she looked out into the night at the Ganges River, made her feel completely at peace.

> **Figuring out how you can change anything that's not getting you where you want to be is a good way to get where you're going.**

She eventually made it back to the States, but she remembered that moment of feeling completely content with her life. She would check in with that revelation every few months. Could she still say that she was happy with the way she was living and was moving toward where she wanted to be?

It's a good gut check. It's one I'm learning to make from time to time. Is this the life I would choose, not changing a thing? If there is something I'd change, what is that? What steps can I take to fix it?

Figuring out how you can change anything that's not getting you where you want to be is a good way to get where you're going.

And if you don't want to change anything, what a moment to be grateful!

I was reminded of this the other day as I was watching *The Oprah Winfrey Show* on the treadmill, as I do most afternoons. For one particular segment, Winfrey—a Grindhopping sort who started her own production company in her early 30s—let the audience interview her. Someone submitted this question: "If you could walk in someone else's shoes for a week, whose shoes would those be?"

Winfrey laughed and said she'd like to walk in her own shoes in the "right" size, a joke about her constant struggle with her weight.

But then she shook her head. She has a great life, she told the audience. The subtext: this billionaire who was born in poverty has often said that she doesn't believe in luck. She knew where she was going as a young woman. She made plans to get there and has pretty much arrived. Why would she want to be anyone else?

If you can say you wouldn't prefer anyone else's life to your own, chances are you're on the Socorro road. Even if you'll get there ten minutes before dark.

GRINDHOPPING
GUIDELINE #3:

RECALCULATE RISK
How to get comfortable
with being uncomfortable

> *"The easy way is efficacious and speedy, the hard way arduous and long. But, as the clock ticks, the easy way becomes harder and the hard way becomes easier. And as the calendar records the years, it becomes increasingly evident that the easy way rests hazardously upon shifting sands, whereas the hard way builds solidly a foundation of confidence that cannot be swept away."*
> —*Colonel Harland Sanders (1890–1980)*

I came upon this, my favorite quote, during a visit to the first Kentucky Fried Chicken in Corbin, Kentucky. Called the Sanders Café, this spot on U.S. Highway 25 marks the site where the colonel first concocted his secret blend of 11 herbs and spices. Now the restaurant houses a KFC and a shrine to Colonel Sanders. It's got exhibits and photos—and quotes like this one.

Harland Sanders did not have an easy or comfortable life. His father died when he was six. His mother had to work to support the family, which left Harland with cooking duties. He excelled at them. But he did not immediately see how to turn cooking into a profitable career choice. At age 10, he started working at a nearby farm for $2 a month. He left home at age 12 to take a job on a farm in Greenwood, Indiana. Over the next few decades, he tried every trade imaginable, becoming a streetcar conductor in New Albany, Indiana, an army private serving in Cuba, a railroad fireman, a practicing lawyer in justice of the peace courts, an insurance salesman, an Ohio

River steamboat ferry operator, a tire salesman, and a service station owner.

Finally, at age 40, he lit upon the idea of serving meals to his service station customers. Folks enjoyed the grub as it was, but Sanders wasn't satisfied. He spent nine years perfecting his specialty, known as Original Recipe chicken.

Alas, despite its near-addictive chicken, the Sanders Café ran into roadblocks. In the 1950s, the federal government constructed a new interstate highway through Kentucky. The highway bypassed Corbin and, hence, the colonel's restaurant. In anticipation of seeing his business flop, Sanders auctioned off the café, paid his bills, and wound up living on $105 Social Security checks.

Most people, upon losing everything at age 65, would spend the rest of their lives muttering in their rocking chairs. But not Sanders. He seems to have stared rock bottom in the face and decided that it wasn't so bad. Giving up on the chicken he'd spent nine years perfecting, however, didn't sound good at all. So he kept taking the hard way to see what came of it.

He began traveling around the country. He'd drive to a restaurant and cook his Original Recipe chicken for the owner; if the owner liked it, Sanders would let him sell the greasy goods. The owner would then pay Sanders a nickel for every chicken sold. Fast food was taking off in America. Kentucky Fried Chicken, as Sanders's creation came to be known, took off too. By 1964, Sanders had 600 franchises selling his poultry. That year, he sold his stake for $2 million (about $12 million in 2006 dollars). That left him plenty of cash to enjoy the easy way for the rest of his life.

Colonel Sanders is known more for his deep-fried chicken than for his deep thoughts. His quote about taking the hard way was primarily a plea for running an honest business. But his thoughts stuck with me four years after I visited Corbin, when I decided to do something crazy: move to New York City with no job or prospects of one.

I was 23. My year-long internship at *USA Today*, just outside Washington, D.C., was ending, and nobody was clamoring to hire me. So I started asking, "What did I want to be when I grew up?" I wanted to be a writer. But I didn't want to follow the standard route of covering cops and courts for a small-town newspaper in the middle of nowhere. I'd grown up in a small town in the middle of nowhere, and I had no desire to repeat the experience. I wanted to live in New York. At the time, I thought that meant that I needed to hunt for a job with the title "writer" at a New York–based company. I had no idea how I would make that happen. So I spent some of the money I'd saved by eating Ramen during my year of penury and went to Asia for three weeks to contemplate this and other matters.

While I was there, my travel companion's cell phone rang. I'd mentioned to a friend that I might go in with her on an apartment in Manhattan. She went looking and found one, and she wanted to know if she should sign. It was $2,075 a month for the two of us, a terrifying level given that my previous take-home base pay had been $1,200 a month. I'd be putting myself on the hook for a year without any guarantee I'd even bring in that much. But I took a deep breath and said yes.

Risk, I decided, has two sides. There are the risks of what might happen if you do take the hard way and act on your ambitions. I knew what those risks were. I might wind up broke, squeegee-cleaning windshields or, more likely, teaching SAT prep classes. That didn't sound as bad to me as Colonel Sanders living on his $105 Social Security checks. If the worst happened, I'd deal with it.

The risks of *not* acting, however, didn't sound good at all. Over time, as Colonel Sanders said, the easy way becomes harder. Perhaps I could have moved back home with my parents. I could have tried to find a small-town newspaper or magazine job or something in corporate communications. I wouldn't have been happy, but at least I would have had a paycheck. I could have enrolled in a journalism master's degree program to put the whole job thing off for a year while I racked up debt for the privilege. But all those things would have just put me farther away from my goal of being a writer living in New York. If I didn't move when I was young enough to have a whole binder of Ramen recipes, it might never happen. And that downside was worse than the squeegee one.

As Sanders predicted, the hard way was arduous at first. Scratch that. Grind-free living was *terrifying*. I stepped off the train on September 2, 2002, humming that line from *Annie* about having "three bucks, two bags, one me." Okay, I had a bit more than $3, but not a lot. I had no furniture. I'd lie on the living room floor and scribble questions in my journal like, "What the hell am I doing with my life?" I had a lot of dizzy spells. It was uncertainty gone psychosomatic.

I'm glad I stuck it out, though, because risking that dizziness turned out to be the best decision of my life. I celebrate my "New York birthday" every year on September 2. It sounds cheesy, but I like to remember how enamored I soon became with my new home. I would marvel at the corner delis selling blue flowers at all hours of the night. Blue flowers at 2 a.m.! White flowers, I could see. But blue was an extravagance. I laughed at a man selling flags on September 10, 2002, yelling, "They're $2 today. They'll be $3 tomorrow!" And as I fell in love with the city, the city showered gifts on me. Writing projects kept coming my way until I realized I didn't need a "job." I'd always loved to sing; moving to New York meant I got to sing in Carnegie Hall with one of the community choirs I joined. I even met my husband in a bar in Greenwich Village and married him almost two years to the day after I took New Jersey Transit into the city and sat there wondering what I was supposed to do next.

Given how well the New York move turned out, I've become an even bigger fan of the Colonel Sanders quote. The hard way does get easier over time. Some Grindhoppers are gamblers and some are not. Most, though, have told me that they evaluate risk with these questions in mind:

- **What is the worst that can happen if I *don't* take the hard way?**

- **What is the worst that can happen if I do?**

- **Is the worst that can happen if I stretch myself really all that bad?**

- **What is the upside of taking this risk?**

- **What can I do to hedge against the downside?**

I did a few things on that last front. I had some money in the bank. I knew that *USA Today* would continue to print my columns. During my last month at the newspaper, I'd also freelanced for enough other places that I'd more than doubled my salary. So I suspected that I could replace my paycheck. I moonlighted a few hours a week assisting a travel marketing entrepreneur with her projects until I was hired to cowrite a book. When you set out for unknown seas, it's good to have a few lifejackets on board.

But ultimately, you still have to set sail. The first four questions help you be rational about it so that you can enjoy the sea breezes on the journey.

Mena Trott, cofounder with her husband Ben of the blogging software company Six Apart, shares this philosophy. "It's important not to be fearful of things," she says. "It's easy enough to recover from minor mistakes that you don't have to be paralyzed into not doing anything."

Mena and Ben met as high school students in Sonoma County, California. She liked design and writing, but thought she'd be a lawyer because her father was one and she liked to argue. Ben was the class valedictorian and very shy. Mena was a troublemaker and "wasn't the best student. I wasn't interested in what they were teaching us. But I was interested in Ben. I decided to marry him on the spot."

A few years later, she did. The two went to work for a dot-com. Then they got laid off. Like me, they then took a big risk because the easy options weren't appealing. Quite simply, "We didn't want to have to go and get another job."

Mena had been keeping a blog during all this. She didn't like the available Web publishing tools, so the two decided to give themselves a few months to develop new software that they'd share with friends. "We never really planned on its being a start-up when we did it," Mena says of Six Apart, which takes its name from the space in days between Ben's and her birth dates. "We did it purely as a hobby." If people liked the software, they said, well, the Trott Rent Fund was taking donations.

They launched Movable Type version 1.0 on October 8, 2001. One hundred people downloaded it in the first hour. Over the next few months, the speed of downloading increased, and the money sent in to thank them actually did pay the couple's rent. Since they were only in their mid-20s and had some savings, they were doing all right. But that summer they had to make another big decision. Ben was offered a "good" stable job. Should they go with the easy way and its steady paychecks, or stick with the 70-hour, underpaid weeks?

In the end, they decided to commit themselves to Six Apart. The two had been working by themselves out of their apartment for so long that they resisted hiring other people. But soon the growth in demand for their software left them little choice. An investor dragged them to his office in Japan to tell them why they needed funding. They agreed. Their head count began to rise. Six Apart now employs 130 people and is on target to hit 165 when this book hits stores. Its blogging products let various online oracles—like *Dilbert* creator Scott Adams—share their random thoughts with readers. And like the lawyer she might have been, Mena gets to argue at technology conventions about blogging manners and the hidden dangers of the TrackBack feature that she helped develop.

Along the way, she's made her peace with the easy way vs. hard way calculation. What's the worst that could happen? "If this company failed tomorrow—God forbid—I'd still feel like I've learned so much that I couldn't have learned otherwise at the next stage of my career after [the first company they worked for] failed," she says.

THE RISKS OF THE EASY WAY

Working hard in pursuit of uncertain future rewards of the kind that Six Apart might deliver is a risk. But so is working hard in pursuit of uncertain future rewards at a big company.

Given corporate America's epidemic of layoffs, restructurings, pension freezes, and pension discharges and the decreasing number of jobs as you get higher up the pyramid, I'm not sure you can bank on any future rewards with a real job beyond your next paycheck.

> **Given corporate America's epidemic of layoffs, restructurings, pension freezes, and pension discharges and the decreasing number of jobs as you get higher up the pyramid, I'm not sure you can bank on any future rewards with a real job beyond your next paycheck.**

Because they make that calculation, I think Grindhoppers have a better sense of risk than most people working in the grind.

When I started freelancing, the risks of doing so appeared in all their glory. I never knew when the next check would arrive. I took a two-week vacation during the summer of 2003 and, as a net result, took in a grand total of $400 one month. That just about covered my utilities and health insurance premium—and nothing else. Thankfully, that month of famine was followed by a five-figure feast month. But the whole experience left me reeling.

So, to help myself become comfortable with the risks and uncertainty of my life, I started keeping a list that would remind me that real jobs have risks, too. I call this the "Wow, I'm glad I freelance" file. I recommend compiling such a stack of articles or e-mails (you might call it the "Wow, I'm glad I started my own company" file or the "Wow, I'm glad I quit my job" file) to anyone carving an unconventional career path.

One of the benefits of being a freelance writer, for instance, is surfing the Web merrily, often pointlessly, for hours in the guise of "research."

A recent *BusinessWeek* article, however, noted that a growing number of companies are monitoring and restricting their employees' Web use. The magazine reported that Kozy Shack Enterprises of Hicksville, New York, uses the "quota time" feature in a program called Websense Enterprise to give employees one hour a day to browse. Managers can choose what sites are available during that time and adjust access depending on job titles. The company's IT director noted that "We have sales people who travel extensively, so we give them much more access to travel sites."

I'm sure they appreciate that.

Also in the file: in 2005, the California Supreme Court found itself dealing with a fascinating retaliation case called *Yanowitz v. L'Oreal USA*. Elysa Yanowitz, a regional sales manager for L'Oreal, sued the company in 1999, claiming that visiting manager John Wiswall told her that a saleswoman at the Macy's store in Santa Clara's Valley Fair Mall was "not good looking enough" and to fire her and "get me somebody hot." When Wiswall returned later to find that Yanowitz hadn't fired the saleswoman (because the saleswoman sold a lot of products, and because Yanowitz thought it would be illegal to fire someone based on looks), he pointed to a blonde woman and said, "Goddamn it, get me one that looks like that." Yanowitz, who had been named Sales Manager of the Year in 1997, claimed that she soon began receiving bad evaluations. She quit and sued; the case has already taken six years to decide exactly how much of a boor your boss can be in a damned-if-you-do, damned-if-you-don't work environment.

Men don't have a lock on the boorish boss category, by the way. South Carolina–based writer W. Thomas Smith, Jr., tells me that he discovered the little-known white-collar risk of actual physical abuse from a former female boss. She used to sneak up behind him and hit him in the back of the head. Not playfully. "She slapped the crap out of me," he says. Then she would say, "You're a former Marine. You're tough. You can take it." Sure. But in actual military situations, you're often allowed to strike *back*.

Then there are the risks to your sanity. Freelancer Ruth Laney once worked for a nonprofit where a buzzer on the wall of her office sounded every time the front door opened or shut. "It went off about 80 times a day," she says. She asked to have it shut off and was told that it was there for "security" purposes. "This was in an office full of people, with the door opening and shutting constantly. I lasted seven months. It's hard to believe it wasn't seven hours."

Many of the items on outplacement firm Challenger, Gray & Christmas's list of "The Most Unbelievable Workplace Events of 2005" also landed in the file. My favorite: "A woman says she was suspended from her job for spending too much time trying to rescue a squirrel trapped in the ceiling of the library where she works."

A close runner-up: "A German company initiated a strict no-whining policy. Negative Nellies and other boat rockers are under a two-moans-and-out rule. According to the company, several workers have quit and two others have been fired for violating the whine-free policy."

On a more serious note, though, we've all met downsized 45-year-old professionals who are scrambling to find work at a salary approaching their previous pay. They face all the hassles of starting new jobs, such as younger bosses and vacation days that start accruing only after you've worked a whole year. It's sad when someone gets a grand two months of severance after years of service. It's even sadder when the person has moved her family because of a transfer, put in late nights and weekends, and canceled vacations and such because her supervisor said that a project needed to be finished *now*. And then, at a moment's notice and with a supervised desk cleaning, she's out.

When you work for someone else, it's tempting to make sacrifices in anticipation of some future payoff. But in light of our layoff-happy economy, giving up something that you truly do want—like your free time, your youth, or your health—for a tentative future payoff is a huge risk. The downside of lost years or lost happiness means that real jobs can be more risky than starting your own business or juggling the multiple clients that most freelancers maintain. There are some upsides to real jobs. I do know people who love their jobs with an all-consuming passion, have worked for the same company for years, and are paid well in money, perks, and flexibility for their tenacity. But I challenge you to find many of those lucky ducks.

Interview Gen-X workers who are worried about layoffs, says Bruce Tulgan, author of *Winning the Talent Wars*, and "They say, 'I'm too conservative to pay my dues and climb the ladder.' . . . The irony is that this is the new, adult, security-seeking behavior."

So Grindhopping is *conservative*? It's certainly harder to strike out on your own. But as Colonel Sanders tells us, the easy way becomes harder and the hard way becomes easier over time. Or as one Grindhopper puts it, "Every single day, you will wonder if you're doing the right thing, especially when you're broke, stressed, exhausted, and feel you've lost all your friends . . . but at least you're not semi-broke and sitting in a cubicle, wishing you had the balls to go out there and be broke, stressed, exhausted, and losing all your friends. . . . Right?"

Right.

THE RISKS OF THE HARDER WAY

It's hard to recalculate risk rationally, though, with some of the alarming numbers out there.

You've probably seen the statistic floating around that "According to the Small Business Administration, 50 percent of start-ups fail in the first year, and 95 percent fail within five." It's a daunting figure, though it's less daunting when you learn that, in the words of SBA spokesman John McDowell, "the oft-quoted statistics are bogus."

According to a study by Amy E. Knaup in the May 2005 *Monthly Labor Review*, about 80 percent of new establishments "born" in the second quarter of 1998 were still in existence a year later. Two-thirds (66 percent) were still around to celebrate their second birthday, and 44 percent were still in existence after four years.

That's not a huge number, but it's also important to note that a business closure does not mean a business failure. There were 576,200 small business closures in 2004, the SBA notes, but only

> "You've probably seen the statistic floating around that 'According to the Small Business Administration, 50 percent of start-ups fail in the first year, and 95 percent fail within five.' It's a daunting figure, though it's less daunting when you learn that, in the words of SBA spokesman John McDowell, 'the oft-quoted statistics are bogus.'"

34,317 bankruptcies. In many of the other cases, the owner retired, sold the space, or moved on to a different project.

These statistics are far more encouraging than the nattering nabobs would lead you to believe. They also refer to small businesses with employees and, hence, higher cash-flow needs. Many Grindhoppers start what could best be called microbusinesses, which employ only the Grindhopper herself. Talking about "failure" for these microbusinesses makes little sense. If a freelance photographer decides to reenter the grind because a magazine offers her a full-time salary that she thinks is a good deal, that doesn't mean that her freelance photography business failed. Freelancers tend to have good years and bad years (which may require moonlighting; see Grindhopping Guideline 4), but it's not too hard to have revenues top costs when you have no one but yourself to pay.

That said, it's worth looking at what makes Grindhopping stints explode in the kind of fantastic way we all fear.

Kaleil Isaza Tuzman had some experience with this. In the late 1990s, he cofounded govWorks.com, a service that allowed people to pay government fees online. Despite its minimal revenue at the time, Isaza Tuzman and his partners raised $60 million in venture capital. The company zoomed from a handful of employees to about 200 in a year. Then the company went from being worth millions, with 200 employees, to being bankrupt in about another year. You can see the fast fall in the 2001 documentary *Startup.com*.

Plenty of other dot-com boy wonders experienced the same thing. During my internship at *Fortune* magazine during the summer of 2000, one of my tasks was to help evaluate the net worth of the 40 richest Americans under age 40. In 2000, you needed a paper net worth of at least $400 million to make the top 40 cut. By 2004, a bit over $100 million would do—and not because all the original rich pups had aged out of the bracket.

That's a lot of lost wealth.

So I, too, thought that most new enterprises failed, until I did some research on "Mompreneurs," or high-achieving moms who hop out of the grind to do their own thing. After delving into this universe of home-based massage therapists, start-up publishers, ice cream franchise owners, yacht operators, construction company presidents, and mom-and-baby exercise video producers, I've decided that spectacular start-up failures have something in common.

They're run by men—a certain kind of men.

Now, don't get me wrong. Men have started spectacularly successful businesses, too, some of the Grindhopping sort profiled in this book. But it's also men who built the big hierarchies of corporate America. The type A male business temperament likes to run an empire. Many young male entrepreneurs idolize men like that, and so they try to build their own empires by borrowing or raising a lot of money at the beginning and getting big quick—far quicker than demand would justify. These would-be empire builders hire people because they like to be in charge of people, not because their growth rates justify doing so. Many also fall into the trap of taking themselves very seriously. I've met few women entrepreneurs in the course of this research who called themselves "CEO" when they had one part-time employee who was actually a family member pitching in on weekends. It was the rare male entrepreneur who *didn't*.

Title worship is fine, if silly. We all like to show off our peacock feathers from time to time. But problems arise when you start acting like the CEO of a multimillion-dollar corporation before you've even hit six figures of revenue. You wind up with bills you can't pay, which makes your investors' money disappear faster than David Copperfield.

Moms, on the other hand, rarely fall into this trap. That makes them excellent entrepreneurs. They're as patient with their businesses as they are with small, shrieking children. They choose less capital-intensive ventures, and they try not to borrow much money to start. They're very careful with budgets. After all, they usually start businesses to combine work and family, not to hurt the family because of their work. Most have to be dragged into hiring people as demand expands. They get bigger as their children become more independent. That happens over years, not weeks, which is a good time frame for business growth.

It's also a good plan for business success. Some mompreneurs become so successful that their husbands quit their jobs and go to work for them.

Ellen Parlapiano and Patricia Cobe, authors of the book *Mompreneurs* (and holders of the trademark on that word), back me up on this.

Parlapiano reports that they were researching a sequel to that book, called *Mompreneurs Online*, when the dot-com bubble burst. A year later, they went back to their subjects, expecting to count

71

casualties. To their surprise, while plenty of tech companies had exploded, "every single one of these women entrepreneurs was still in business."

It turns out that there's a difference between selling scrapbooking albums and stickers that you design on an Internet craft portal, and buying an album-making factory and hiring 25 people to fill orders in advance of the first purchase.

You are highly unlikely to fail with the first method. You are spectacularly likely to fail with the second. So if you don't want to fail, try idolizing Henry Ford a bit less and your soccer mom neighbor with the home-based accounting business a bit more.

BUSINESSES WOBBLE; GRINDHOPPERS DON'T

All this talk of failure, though, misses the bigger point. When you're young, there aren't many practical downsides of stretching yourself. Bright, ambitious people, like cats, tend to land on their feet.

When I caught up with Kaleil Isaza Tuzman in 2004 for a *Reader's Digest* profile, he'd gotten up from the wreckage of govWorks and reemerged as the president and managing partner of Recognition Group, a corporate restructuring firm. He speaks at various entrepreneurship conferences, has designed a multimedia Entrepreneur's Success Kit, and has raised over $150 million for various investments.

> **All this talk of failure misses the bigger point. When you're young, there aren't many practical downsides of stretching yourself. Bright, ambitious people, like cats, tend to land on their feet.**

In other words, he's doing fine.

Since most career bumps in the road aren't nearly so dramatic, they tend to turn out all right for entrepreneurial types who don't have movies made about their ventures, too.

Jeremy Kestler started his post-MBA career in a colorless, windowless office at Coca-Cola where "it took ten minutes to describe where I was in the corporate expanse."

This was the late 1990s. Dot-coms were calling. So he quit and went to work for one. Then he got laid off. He found a job at another dot-com. Then he got laid off again. During the stint of unemployment and the stint as a small business counselor at a Georgia college that followed, he decided to invent a product to solve a problem that had long vexed him: there is no good way to store laundry and transport it from small apartments or dorms to the Laundromat.

Clothes hampers and laundry baskets take up floor space and are tough to carry. You can hang a mesh drawstring laundry bag in the closet, but such bags have a design flaw: the more you stuff in, the smaller the opening at the top becomes.

So Kestler went to a fabric store, found a bulletin board posting from a seamstress who did piecework, and hung out in her basement for the next few months, constructing a backpackish contraption that he called the LaundraPak. It's made from durable, water-resistant fabric. You load it up as it hangs over a closet door. Then you carry it on your back to the machines.

Kestler has had some success with the product. More than 50 college bookstores sell it. In his small business counselor role, he learned that the QVC television shopping network was holding an audition nearby, looking for the next big thing. He showed up with his LaundraPak and waited in line with Rube Goldbergs carrying inventions of all varieties (a six-foot planter, a coffee table with a surge protector . . .). He earned a spot hawking it on the air. He sold 200 units.

Unfortunately, QVC required him to have at least 1,200 units on hand, which meant an outlay of several thousand dollars more than he took in. A contract with a big-box store didn't pan out as expected, and with his wife needing to move to New Jersey for her job, Kestler decided to put the LaundraPak toward the bottom of the hamper for a while. He also decided he needed to do something that provided a steadier income.

So he undertook the most old-fashioned job search imaginable. He put on a suit, grabbed a leather folder, and went around knocking on doors. He delivered résumés to a few dozen central New Jersey firms. A human resources consulting and training firm offered him a job. He's been working there happily ever since.

When people talk about the risks of creating a career outside big institutions, they're often talking about the risk of losing money. That can happen, though being smart about finances and revenue lessens that risk.

But the bigger risk that ambitious young people worry about is losing years. Grindhoppers are smart kids. They often attended elite colleges with classmates who competed over who earned the most merit badges growing up, who could get the biggest signing bonus out of college, and who could get promoted the fastest. No one wants to show up at his tenth reunion working at an entry-level job at a company after his four start-up attempts failed. That Grindhopper really doesn't want to find out that a classmate who paid his dues has a plum job several ranks up the hierarchy from him in the same company. There's only a small chance that this would happen. A lot of businesses do value entrepreneurial activity as experience. Grindhoppers are well connected and convincing enough to land good jobs when they look. Indeed, many Grindhoppers wouldn't mind entering the corporate world someday, when they're offered positions high above the dues-paying level. Many Grindhoppers do just that.

Still, the question of lost time is a real one for many of us.

Kestler has faced that question head-on. If he'd joined a consulting firm right out of business school, for instance, and stayed with it, he might have made partner by now. Or if he'd stayed at Coke, he could have risen to a place where it wouldn't take ten minutes to describe his job.

"That's the $64,000 question," he told me. If he'd done things differently, perhaps he could have made more money or more career progress.

But that's a big if. Coca-Cola laid off several thousand people at around the time Kestler left. There's no guarantee that he wouldn't have gotten hit in a subsequent round. Plenty of people leave consulting and finance companies long before they reach the upper rungs, which reduces the value proposition for putting in the tough early years that these places require. Kestler had friends from business school who worked for Enron and Arthur Andersen. Needless to say, those folks haven't made as much career progress as they might have, either. "When those types of institutions get torn down around you, you feel like less of a bonehead for taking a risk," Kestler says. "What was previously considered the 'safe' route isn't really as safe as it once was."

Another reason that Grindhoppers need not worry about lost years is the growing phenomenon of adultolescence. Plenty of people who *do* want jobs in the grind still have no idea what they're doing with their lives at age 30. I spoke with a 30-year-old recently who was in the middle of a potentially decade-long PhD program, but hadn't yet pondered what he wanted to do with that degree.

Maybe he'll earn another one. The "education is good" mantra that we've been hearing all these years has produced a new breed of achiever: the degree collector. Recruiters can tell you about job seekers who have earned a college degree, then a law degree, then a master's degree in public health, then started a PhD program, then switched to an MBA—and then what? Like drug addicts after the next hit, these people believe that the next degree will lead to the perfect job and the perfect life. They don't realize that no credential on earth can hand you happiness.

A Grindhopper who tries the entrepreneurial life for a decade, fails, then goes to law school will still be starting a stable, grown-up existence before someone who won't jump off the degree train. Colonel Sanders didn't hit his stride until he qualified for Social Security. And with his face on billboards everywhere from Beijing, China, to Seville, Spain, he's certainly done better than anyone acting snooty at your tenth reunion.

OH, AND YOU MIGHT SUCCEED, TOO

When you're young, the risks of failure are relative. We live in an economy where it's easy for young people to start over. As Jeremy Kahn of Oral Fixation Mints puts it, "In my opinion, it's not much of a risk at this stage at all. . . . As long as you have food on the table and a roof to sleep under, you're fine." If you have only yourself to support, it's possible to produce food and a roof under the austerity plan (see Grindhopping Guideline 1) by making lattes for 25 hours a week at Starbucks and doing some SAT prep tutoring at night.

The nature of risk, though, is that big risks carry big rewards. Striking out on your own carries upsides that few people stuck in the grind can match.

You might get rich, for instance. Two 30-something guys named Larry and Sergey in Mountain View, California, can tell you about this. Just make sure you catch them before they board the Boeing 767 they bought around the time Google stock hit $400 last year.

You don't have to make billions, though, to do well. The National Association for the Self-Employed reports that the average self-employed worker earns slightly more than the average wage-earning or salaried worker. Two-thirds of the high-net-worth individuals that Thomas Stanley and William Danko studied in their book *The*

Millionaire Next Door were self-employed. The Census Bureau's 1997 Current Population Survey found that 5 percent of self-employed workers earned over $100,000 in 1996; only 3 percent of other workers did. That may not sound like a huge difference, but if I were the kind of person who wrote all-caps press release headlines, I'd point out that "SELF-EMPLOYED PEOPLE ARE 67 PERCENT MORE LIKELY TO EARN SIX FIGURES THAN THEIR GRIND-BOUND PEERS!"

When you work for yourself, your income rises based on how much business you can drum up, not what a salary scale dictates you're worth.

The rewards aren't just monetary, either. One of the greatest joys of free agency is gaining control of your time. In a recent Freelancers Union study of New York City independent workers, 86 percent said that having a "flexible schedule" was one of the main advantages of this lifestyle. It's certainly a big plus for me. Freelancing has given me the chance to write books, train for half-marathons, sing in my choirs, and travel four to six weeks each year. Grindhoppers with kids speak of the joys of experiencing small moments—like catching fireflies with their kids on summer evenings if they choose to—when most people are still commuting. Maybe there's more risk in such decisions. You have to take the hard way, not the easy way. You have to become comfortable with being uncomfortable. But the results can make all the risks worthwhile.

> **When you work for yourself, your income rises based on how much business you can drum up, not what a salary scale dictates you're worth.**

GRINDHOPPING
GUIDELINE #4:

THINK PROJECTS, *NOT* JOBS
Welcome to the Craig's List Economy

Young people have always felt angst about their life choices. Jane Austen's novels chronicle the panic that 20-something women once felt about finding husbands. Now that angst is more career-oriented. Writing today, Austen might observe that it is a truth universally acknowledged that a college senior who is soon to be in possession of a diploma but not of a grad school acceptance letter must be in want of a job.

Sometime in the fall of my senior year of college, I experienced that angst firsthand. Being the practical sort, I journeyed to the career services office to learn some job-hunting techniques. There, I learned that landing a job requires a snazzy résumé. I did a little research on résumé formats on the Internet. That's when I discovered the great commandments of résumé writing.

These appear to have been handed down on stone tablets from human resources executives thousands of years ago. They are drilled like the Word of God into job seekers' heads.

As a college senior, I tried to familiarize myself with all of them. For instance, I learned that my résumé needed an "objective." That seemed odd to me, since, obviously, I was trying to get a reporting job with my résumé, which was why I was sending it to people who said they were hiring entry-level reporters at newspapers. But just in case, I put something unconvincing about seeking a reporting job. I caught sight of fancier-looking résumés in my dorm's printer and redid mine with a bold horizontal line below my address and bullet points by my accomplishments. To keep everything on one page, I shrank my print size to something that was either sophisticated or myopia-inducing, depending on your prescription. And I made sure to put in lots of numbers. Instead of "spent summer writing bylined articles for the *Washington Times*," I put "spent summer writing 30 bylined articles." Before I put in the numbers, I got no job offers. After I put in the numbers, I still got no job offers. But I'm sure the recruiters were impressed that I followed the rules!

When you're a 21-year-old kid, though, you're not expected to have a stunning résumé. It's when you've been in the workforce for a while that things get complicated. If you create a "chronological résumé," you are supposed to demonstrate a history of continuous employment. Job seekers become quite fundamentalist about this point. I have seen posts on job boards saying, "I was out of work for two months; is that going to look bad on my résumé?" as if some almighty résumé deity decreed that cubicle time must be clocked to the hour. Then someone follows up with a question on whether it's best to suffer miserably at a job so that your résumé shows you stayed put for a year. You don't want to look like a job hopper. Job hoppers are the career equivalent of lepers.

There are, of course, ruses to disguise your leprosy. If you haven't been continuously employed, or if you have an incarceration record, which résumé books tend to treat as the same thing, you are told to create a "skills-based" resume. This lists attributes like "hard working" and provides evidence. Example: "Worked more overtime shifts at prison canteen than any other inmate" or "Wrote 60,000-word books annually."

As it is, my senior-year job search taught me a valuable lesson about résumés—that is, they're not that valuable at all. I found my first job not with a résumé, but by convincing someone I'd met who had the ability to get me an internship at *USA Today* to get me that internship. Now, as a freelancer, I occasionally update my résumé on my Web site for giggles. But the truth is, almost no one asks me for it. People ask me to do projects because they've seen my work. Or someone else who's seen my work recommends me. Or I call someone up and say I can meet a need she has.

Which leads me to the new "résumé" rules that Grindhoppers discover along the way.

First, by the time you're sending a résumé to HR, you're toast. The chance that your one-page chronological or skill-based list will wiggle through the keyword filters and survive some bureaucrat's idea of a good candidate is nil.

Even if you've got a stunning résumé, the HR route can lose you big bucks. Many companies insist that your résumé list salary requirements, thereby compelling you to forfeit any advantage you might have in the negotiation process. And most jobs get filled with people known to the company long before you hear about them. That makes sense. I'd prefer to hire someone I know and like than someone dredged up by a résumé cattle call. Wouldn't you?

> **By the time you're sending a résumé to HR, you're toast. The chance that your one-page chronological or skill-based list will wiggle through the keyword filters and survive some bureaucrat's idea of a good candidate is nil.**

Second, all this fuss about listing jobs in order, with dates showing no gaps, or inventing elaborate ruses to cover said gaps assumes that we're living in a world where people have one job at a time and one job for a long time. At any moment, I have at least four projects of varying lengths clogging my desk. What résumé form should that take? Where do I list my dates? It makes no sense. I've wound up just listing "Current projects" at the top of my résumé and highlighting random past lives below.

An increasing number of young people now inhabit this more free-flowing version of a labor market. It's a little more chaotic than the days that the old résumé rules were designed for. But that's a good thing.

In the past few decades, the industrial world's capital markets have become incredibly flexible. If you want to borrow money to buy a house, finance an education, or buy that too-cute Coach clutch at Macy's, you can, at rather reasonable rates. If you want to buy stock, you can buy shares within pennies of the price you see quoted on

...JNBC as you e-mail your broker. If you want to take all your money out of stocks and put it in gold, this can be (mostly) accomplished in the 40 minutes' warning you have before the nuclear bomb hits.

But if you decide you no longer want to be in advertising, but instead would like to be in finance, there is no clear-cut path for switching. People will transfer their credit card balances from a card they don't like far quicker than they'll quit a job they don't like. Your first dollar in an investment looks the same as the last dollar in. No one can say that about the employees in a company.

That's fine. People aren't money. But the result of this premium put on long-term stability is that the labor market is quite inefficient. Talented people don't know about good jobs. Hiring managers don't know about the best candidates. Bad people stay in jobs when there are far better people out there, just because it's a pain in the ass to fire the first guy and find someone else. If you want to make money, but you want to quit after a few weeks or you want to take two-month vacations, traditionally, temping has been your only choice.

Fortunately, this is changing. We are entering what I call the "Craig's List Economy."

Founded in 1995 by San Francisco native and IT guy Craig Newmark, Craig's List is a mostly free online classifieds section for jobs, stuff, and love. If you've never visited the site (www.craigslist.org, then follow the links to your city), you should check it out. Then pick up this book again tomorrow after you've spent the night pondering why the 45-year-old guy in Memphis is selling both a wedding dress and an inflatable doll.

After you've gotten over the shock value, though, check out the job and project listings. Some are for full-time positions, but others offer $60 for help moving for a morning, or $100 to pose for an afternoon art seminar. There's no formality to it at all. You e-mail if you're interested, or you post a note offering your services and agree on a reasonable rate with the other person. No HR department or résumé filters are necessary. You do the job. You get paid. Then you move on with your life, or work together again if you're so inclined.

Many of the jobs on Craig's List are for low dollar amounts and low skill levels. I'm not suggesting that you can make a great living doing $100-a-day gigs. But the principle is being carried over into the broader economy.

We have projects now, not jobs.

When Grindhoppers work with clients, they do so on mutually agreeable terms for as long as both are satisfied. Both are free to move on at any time, and neither approaches the deal with the weight of payroll taxes, pensions, benefits, or a full-time commitment that precludes earning money from other sources. If Grindhoppers run small businesses, each product line or customer could be considered a project; if Grindhoppers freelance, they usually work on projects for several clients at once.

Sure, some employers abuse this. Though it's dodgy in legal terms, there are places that call employees "independent contractors" and still make them show up onsite 40 hours or more a week. That's not Grindhopping. That's a grind. Even worse, it's a grind without subsidized health insurance. That lack of benefits is a major reason you see some social critics complaining about the rise in self-employment among young people. They cite stats like a February 2005 study from the Bureau of Labor Statistics that found that 55 percent of contingent workers would have preferred a permanent job.

But there are problems with using this statistic to damn the Craig's List Economy. The BLS defines contingent workers as persons who do not expect their jobs to last. That's really most of us *except* the self-employed these days. Furthermore, the BLS does not include most self-employed workers or microbusiness owners in its definition of contingent workers; only 3 percent of independent contractors met the BLS "contingent" standard. The same BLS study found that 82 percent of independent contractors preferred their alternative work arrangements to more traditional options.

Critics also err in thinking that you can obtain affordable health insurance only through employers, or that people aren't willing to trade subsidized health insurance for freedom (see "Dealing with the Downsides" for more on this). Most of the people profiled in this book have been quite happy to make that trade. They know that the relationship between Grindhoppers and their clients or customers is more even than the relationship between employers and employees has ever been. Only 9 percent of independent contractors told the BLS that they'd prefer to be in the grind.

The principle of diversifying can apply to both investments and income. When you start thinking projects, not jobs, you never worry about résumé gaps again.

Even people who mostly work in the grind are discovering that the old résumé rules were written for a different era. They know that

> **The principle of diversifying can apply to both investments and income. When you start thinking projects, not jobs, you never worry about résumé gaps again.**

few employers offer lifetime commitments. So they, likewise, treat their full-time jobs as projects, to be chosen on their merits and discarded when they no longer meet their needs.

For the past few years, I've been following one young man's career as he's been doing just that. He's committed every résumé sin in the book. He worked for Amazon for a while, quit because he burned out, and spent two months living in his car at a ski area and doing a lot of backcountry skiing and climbing. When he decided that he'd had his fill of relaxation and needed some cash, he got another e-business job despite that "gap" by explaining to recruiters that, hey, he needed a break. Not only did that admission not hurt him, but he wound up making more money than he had been making before. He made a few more job hops, and then, last fall, left his job at eBay to start a real estate investment company. Six months in, he decided that the real estate market was cooling off and that he also missed living in a city. So he reinserted himself into the job market after another "gap," this time landing a position at Orbitz. Once again, he wound up with a higher salary and more responsibility (he's currently managing six direct reports).

Lucky? Maybe. Or maybe, in this fast-moving new economy, smart employers realize that gaps and job hopping—like leprosy in this age of antibiotics—are not the scourges we once thought they were. People who can cheerfully and efficiently deliver on any objective they're given are worth defying a few old-fashioned rules for. People who push themselves and set their own objectives may justify burning the résumé books. Who cares if the person will sign on for only two years because he plans to spend the year of his thirtieth birthday doing month-long hikes in places like Santiago de Compostela in Spain? He'll still work hard for two years. That's not a benefit to be taken lightly.

The question for Grindhoppers is how to navigate the Craig's List Economy to their advantage. Though this is a new economy, I like to keep a rather old image in mind.

THE MASTODON MINDSET

Phoenix-based Grindhopper Andrew Brooks has a good life. He and his wife take dance lessons (her idea, he swears). He goes for walks with their toddler son and the dogs most days, and he runs long distances with the Arizona mountains as inspirational scenery. He often works from home on his life management company, Maximum Balance (www.maximumbalance.com). Maximum Balance provides an online meeting spot for people who are interested in achieving balanced lives. The discussion groups and articles help users prioritize activities in what Brooks deems the five main areas of life: Personal, Relationships, Career, Financial, and Giving. To balance his own life and stay exposed to other ideas, he keeps his hand in other software and consulting enterprises through a stake in an incubating company called Mural Ventures.

He also has the ability to run a relay race with me with a bad metaphor.

I interviewed Brooks in his life-balance-guru capacity to ask for tips for this chapter. Lacking Stephen Covey's motivational seminar gift for apt allusions, I suggested that maybe it was smart to pretend we were cavemen, and that going after big projects was the caveman equivalent of hunting mastodons.

You always want to be hunting a mastodon. That's because mastodons are hard to catch. You don't catch many in a lifetime. Yet they don't last forever. That's a problem, because the old rules for building a career are based on hunting for one mastodon and gnawing on that thing until you retire. You live in fear of gaps between mastodons. If someone moves your mastodon or your caveman tribe merges with another and there's only so much mastodon to go around (stay with me here), or if you decide that your fellow tribe members are losers, or if the mastodon just turns out not to be too tasty, you're left scrambling for more mastodon.

So modern young people, I said, need a smarter mastodon management strategy.

Brooks was wary at first. First of all, did mastodons and humans exist concurrently? Second, was I suggesting that people keep more than one mastodon on hand? "If you look at a lot of entrepreneurial texts, one of the biggest recommendations is to do one thing and make it profitable before you get distracted with other things," he said.

But I assured him that this metaphor was taking place before refrigeration. You can't fit more than one mastodon in your career cave. I just meant that man shouldn't try to live on mastodon alone. And he should be thinking about hunting the next mastodon even as he's eating the first.

"Oh, yes," Brooks said, his voice getting less quizzical. "Even if you've got a mastodon and the best refrigeration, you need the ability to branch out for intellectual and spiritual fulfillment. The act of hunting alone, even if you have a lot of mastodon jerky tucked away, keeps you moving forward. And who knows, maybe someone will pull the plug on that refrigerator and your mastodon will rot."

Grindhoppers realize this need for balance and backup plans. So they pursue smaller projects as they hunt their mastodons. We could think of this as spearing fish, I suggested. Grindhoppers spear fish and gather berries for the time between mastodons.

But all these fish and berries shouldn't be just any fish and berries, Brooks reminded me. "They should be giving you introductions to people who will be customers of your mastodon business. Or they should provide you with new ideas for your mastodon business."

Point taken. And what about those times when things are particularly rough, when you're forced to rely on tree bark and grass for roughage?

"Make sure the things you're doing to stay alive are not pulling you away from capturing the mastodon," he said. "Think about how every project helps build your story and reinforces your plans." In other words, if you've got to eat grass, make sure it's grass on the mastodon-hunting trail.

For Brooks, Maximum Balance is his mastodon. Helping to incubate companies and doing software consulting are his fish and berries. But both are on the mastodon-hunting trail. The executive coaching skills that he refines while incubating small companies pay off in better content and better business strategies for Maximum Balance. The IT consulting helps him brush up on his software skills and gives him ideas for future MB functions. Both bring him into contact with potential customers and partners. And even as he's been chewing on the mastodon of Maximum Balance, he's thinking about the next mastodon. Maybe that would be a series of motivational seminars. Or books.

Likewise, smart Grindhoppers try to follow these new career rules for the Craig's List Economy:

1 **Always be chasing a mastodon (a dream project). Even if you can't eat more than one mastodon at a time, be thinking about the next one while you're chewing.**

2 **Choose fish and berries (good projects) wisely to round out your diet and improve your chances of landing future mastodons.**

3 **Even tree bark (pay-the-bills projects) can keep you on the mastodon path.**

CHASING THE NEXT MASTODON

Brooks is right that trying to eat more than one career mastodon at a time can be trouble. Something must be your top priority. When you become confused about your top priority, you let all your mastodons slip out of your traps. But you can't just depend on your one mastodon, either. It's a tough balancing act. Many of us become tempted to eat two mastodons at once.

Grindhopper Chris Lopinto faced that temptation recently.

Lopinto started his career a few years ago by working at an Internet start-up during college. The company's software product was fairly cool, but fairly pointless, and, sitting in a meeting one day, Lopinto realized that even he didn't see any reason for buying it. The company's demise came not long afterward. So about two months after he graduated, Lopinto suddenly had to figure out something else to do with his life. He didn't want to make the mistake of being left without a mastodon again.

Since he didn't want to work for anyone else, he started an IT consulting company. This was growing well when he stumbled across a better business idea. His uncle had been a Continental Airlines pilot for decades. His father was a 150,000-mile-per-year frequent flyer and knew a lot of the industry's tricks. Lopinto knew how to turn databases of information into user-friendly formats.

So the three of them decided to start ExpertFlyer.com, a subscription service that lets frequent flyers see all the flights going to different destinations, the various available seats, fare buckets, and the probability of upgrading. The service taps the databases that travel agents used before travel agents went the way of the mastodons. ExpertFlyer.com does not sell tickets. That's partly because there's no money in it, and partly to maintain independence.

Lopinto is dedicated to seeing ExpertFlyer taxi down the runway. But he's also had to pay the bills, which is why, when I first interviewed him, he was still running the IT consulting business. "It's tough to split your mind into two different focuses," he told me. Though both ventures have an IT element, elbowing your way into the travel industry involves more schmoozing and hand-holding than consulting. "They're two totally different worlds."

So what do you do? Lopinto's answer was to relegate the IT consulting to fish-and-berry status. When we talked, he wasn't actively seeking new clients (although he wasn't turning them down). He sought ways to do his fish-and-berry business in less time-consuming ways. For instance, many tech problems can be solved remotely, so he tried to do less traveling to client sites.

Relegating projects to fish-and-berry status is often easier said than done, however. When I caught up with Lopinto a few months later, he told me that he'd realized that the ongoing nature of IT support work meant that he couldn't handle the travel schedule necessary to launch ExpertFlyer. So he decided to sell the IT consulting business and focus on his mastodon full-time. For someone who has seen another business go belly-up, relying on one big project is scary. Munching on the mastodon of ExpertFlyer means that he can't tackle any new mastodons. But there is one way to hedge against this situation. If great business ideas pop into Lopinto's head unsought, a common Grindhopping problem, he writes them down for later. This writing-them-down part is crucial to the mastodon mindset. Even though you can't pursue those ideas now, you spend a little time thinking about them, and about how your current project could help you launch these new projects down the line.

After all, you never know when you'll need to hunt for another mastodon. You'll be a step ahead of the game if your last project helps you snag the next one.

Food, spirits, and travel writer Sarah Doyle Lacamoire has found this to be the case. When I interviewed her, she volunteered that she was a Gemini. Those born under the sign of the Twins are known to flit between projects. "I get bored easily," Lacamoire told me. "I'm 29. I've already had four different careers."

Indeed, her résumé flies around to as many places as Lopinto's uncle probably did as a pilot. First, she went to culinary school. Then she worked as an assistant chef. Then she helped produce wedding cakes for a cake company. Then she ran a personal chef business called Sarah, Inc. Then she worked on the launch of TheKnot.com's national magazine, *Weddingpages*, overseeing photo shoots of wedding cakes and writing copy. Then she wrote profiles of restaurants for Zagat's guides and AOL's Digital City. Then she turned all that culinary knowledge and writing experience into a career penning love letters to food. (From *Cooking Light*: "The pumpkin is a master of disguise. Cloaked in cream, eggs or cheese, it cleverly conceals its nutritious bounty in the form of a calorie-packed pie.") When we talked, she had just spent six months in Scotland and had refined that affection into a crush on Scotch. (From the *Boston Globe*: "If the Scotch whisky industry were a man, I would be in love.") She was hunting the mastodon of a longer writing project devoted to her new flame.

> **You never know when you'll need to hunt for another mastodon. You'll be a step ahead of the game if your last project helps you snag the next one.**

Lacamoire's path from chef to editor to Scotch expert was not a clear hunting trail. But if you look more closely, you see that this easily bored Gemini was always thinking about how her current big project could help her spear the next project. When she didn't like working in someone else's restaurant or someone else's cake company, she leveraged her kitchen experience to start a personal chef business. She took her knowledge of food presentation from that gig and decided that she could oversee a magazine's food arrangements. The reporting skills that she learned while writing for and editing the magazine gave her clips for her next big project of becoming a full-time food, spirits, and travel writer.

Lacamoire never waited until a project was done before figuring out where she'd find the next one. When you do that, you won't go too long between mastodons. Even if you're perfectly happy with your gigs at the moment, conditions might change, or new opportunities might present themselves. It pays to know what you'd like to do next.

CHOOSING FISH AND BERRIES

You can't focus on more than one mastodon at a time, but that doesn't mean that you can't run multiple projects. Though this is hard to pull off (as Lopinto discovered), your best bet is to keep one big project as your top priority, and take on others to keep you fed and happy and possibly point you toward your next mastodon. Of such fish and berries is a balanced diet made.

The question to ask, though, is which fish and berries do you pursue?

Pooja Kumar, a former Miss India USA who now works as an actress and model, encounters a number of potential projects in her line of work. Should she do a certain independent film? Or should she audition for a more mainstream TV show? Would this print ad be good for her career? All these projects require investments of time and energy—more specifically, *her* time and energy. In the acting and modeling worlds, you can't hire other people to take on your extra work.

Fortunately, as a shrewd former finance major, Kumar has developed a rubric for judging all her investments of time. It's a good one for those of us in less glamorous careers, too. She asks these questions:

> **Is the project close to my heart? That is, do I feel passionate about the subject matter or think that it will do some good in the world?**

> **Do I respect the people I'll be working with, and trust that they have my best interests at heart?**

> **Will this project help me in the long run?**

Kumar used these questions to evaluate an interesting project she was approached about a few years ago. She had auditioned for Andrew Lloyd Webber's *Bombay Dreams*, but she didn't make the cut ("I'm not a singer," she says). Then the advertising folks called and asked if she wanted to be on the promotional poster for the show. She was confused at first, because, well, she wasn't in the show, which made it a little odd for her to be the poster girl. But the promoters had decided that, with potential cast changes in the future, they simply wanted a beautiful Indian woman in the photo, not the lead actress.

So she ran the opportunity through her three-question rubric. The project was close to Kumar's heart; as the first musical about India to hit Broadway, *Bombay Dreams* would show Americans aspects of Indian culture beyond outsourced call centers. The people working on the show were top-notch. And for a model, it's hard to see how having a giant billboard of your face hanging on 53rd and Broadway for months would hurt your career.

She did the shoots. Sure enough, the results led to opportunities to do other print campaigns. I've gotten stuck behind buses featuring Kumar's face in the ImaginAsian TV channel ads during many a traffic jam.

I like Kumar's questions because they recognize both that time is valuable and that when you're young, you're planning for the long term.

Working on projects that you care about keeps you from burning out. Working with people you respect keeps you from becoming involved in projects that will embarrass you later in life. Thinking about the future, the long run, is what Grindhoppers do best.

Kumar tries to choose projects that earn three "yes" answers. If you don't have lots of projects swimming your way, or if you haven't had the time to track down better berries, maybe you can answer yes to only two of the questions. But personally, I'd start dabbling in the moonlighting list (discussed later in this chapter) before compromising on too many of these fronts.

> **"Working on projects that you care about keeps you from burning out. Working with people you respect keeps you from becoming involved in projects that will embarrass you later in life. Thinking about the future, the long run, is what Grindhoppers do best."**

After you've chosen a project, you should do it well [see Grindhopping Guideline 5, "Seek to Be Judged on Results (and Deliver Them)"]. After you do the project well, though, you're not off the hook. Even if the project wasn't all it was cracked up to be, a little reflection can teach you to make better choices next time.

When Kumar takes a role, she asks afterwards, "Was I true to the character?" and "Did I add something to the character?"—that is, something beyond what the director imagined. She asks if she can take anything she learned as part of that film and implement it in the next one. She asks whether she'd recommend the director and producer. Would she like to work with them again? Then she asks herself what she wants to get out of the next project in light of this last one. Maybe she loved working with people of all ages, for instance, and so she'd like to choose another film that calls for a diverse cast.

When Grindhoppers finish with a project, we all become Geminis. We get bored and want to move on as soon as possible. But a bit of strategizing afterwards can make your next fish and berries far tastier than you anticipated.

DIGESTING GRASSES AND TREE BARK

When you're building a career without paying your dues, sometimes things get rough. Maybe your small business needs more capital than you thought it would to stay operational. Maybe it was a slow month (or four months) for freelance work, and you're gnawing your savings down to the marrow. If so, there's no shame in moonlighting. Plenty of us have done it. Just remember that there's a difference between smart moonlighting (the good grasses and tree bark) and dumb moonlighting (the kind that's best left alone).

First, if you need to take a lousy job, take a lousy job in your industry. There's no point munching on grasses that aren't on the mastodon trail when there are plenty that are. If you want to design your own line of handbags, for instance, and you need extra cash, find a job at a hip, independent boutique. Do not take a job at Barnes & Noble, or at the Gap, for that matter. A corporate chain won't showcase your wares or arrange for sister boutiques in other towns to do so. The owner of a small boutique is probably more plugged in to fashion trends and insiders than a corporate store manager, too.

Second, choose something flexible. Your focus needs to stay on your dream project. If you can't meet with potential clients during the day without losing your job, then your moonlighting won't be getting you closer to your goal.

Third, choose projects that pay more than the minimum wage. If you're taking a job to pay the bills, it should pay the bills. You're a conscientious worker who gets things done smart and fast. Remind yourself that those skills should command a premium, and try to negotiate your rates up. If you would expect to earn $40,000 a year in a full-time job, then don't take gigs that pay less than $20 an hour ($40,000 divided by 50 weeks at 40 hours a week). See Grindhopping Guideline 6 for negotiating tips.

Fourth, think beyond bartending. Ask yourself what services people with excess cash need that you could provide.

Ah, you say. All my friends are as broke as I am. How do I find these people with disposable income? One of the tips in the networking chapter (Grindhopping Guideline 7) is to join religious or civic groups that include people of all ages and income levels, particularly those in tax brackets that your 20-something friends are less likely to inhabit.

If you're living in your hometown, you'll have an advantage here, because you can tap into your parents' network and your friends' parents' networks. Kumar worked precisely that network to get her first roles. Circulate an e-mail describing your services, or post a flyer at your church. Not sure what services to offer? There are several books out there listing home-based jobs for moms or low-capital, part-time jobs for retirees. These jobs are often good ideas for people who aren't moms or retirees, too.

Here are a few Grindhopper-friendly suggestions to get you started:

···> **Try SAT prep, college admissions counseling, essay consulting, and academic tutoring. If you got into a good college, parents tend to assume that you can help their children do the same.**

···> **Think about baby-sitting, elder-sitting, pet-sitting, or providing referrals for all of these. You're not 14 anymore. You can charge more than $5 an hour.**

···> **You can make as much money as people in the grind by doing things that they can't do while they're in the grind. Think along the lines of waiting services (for the plumber or delivery guys) and running errands to places that close by quitting time.**

- **Share your special skills.** If you speak a foreign language, rent yourself out as a conversation partner for people brushing up before a trip abroad. You can give music lessons, give calligraphy lessons, garden, sing at parties, and so on.

- **Prey on people's laziness.** You'd be surprised what people will pay for laundry service, picking up dry cleaning, stitching on buttons or repairing seams, and housecleaning (form a team with a friend and bring your own CDs to make scrubbing fun).

- **Got a sense of style?** Most of us are so style-challenged that you've got options galore. You can make eye-catching scrapbooks or albums for people who aren't sure how to organize their own photos. If you always look smart, you can help people select outfits from their closets or be a shopping consultant. You can gift-wrap packages during the holidays, design gift baskets, hand-write party invitations, or decorate homes for the holidays. You can decorate homes for other times, too, such as when people are selling them and need to create the fantasy that fresh flowers appear in their abodes like manna from heaven.

- **Get rid of stuff for people.** Stage a yard sale for them, or sell their stuff on consignment on eBay. Cruise yard sales for children's clothes, then hold your own sale. If you're organized, organize people's closets and kitchens.

- **Good with design?** Do Web sites, brochures, postcards, and business cards. If you're a stickler for accuracy, proofread résumés, letters, Web site content, and so on.

- **Parties tend to overwhelm their hosts.** You can ease the burden by freelance bartending, baking, cooking, DJ-ing if you know how, or planning children's birthday parties.

····❯ **If you live in a touristy place and you know a lot about it, walking tours can work. Even if you don't live in a touristy place, you can offer relocation assistance to newcomers (think two hours of drive time noting where the best pastry shops are).**

····❯ **Go cruising on Craig's List for administrative jobs, skilled jobs, or random jobs. I just checked the site as I was writing this and found offers to be an extra in a film, test video games, and write copy for real estate brochures.**

····❯ **Substitute teach. Bring Advil and a sense of humor.**

····❯ **Find seasonal work to tide you over between other stints. This could be anything from working in Alaskan canneries to working at political conventions or providing extra mall security during Christmas.**

Whatever you choose, make sure your moonlighting projects keep you focused on your mastodon—your main goal.

Grindhopper Ryan Nerz knew that his main goal was to be a writer and an entertainer. He realized that his premedical path at Yale was unlikely to turn him into either. So he changed tracks, graduated, and tried all sorts of things that would give him a "life worth writing about." He worked briefly as a children's book editor. That wasn't turning him into a writer or entertainer, either. So he quit. Then he needed a new way to support himself as he wrote. So he waited tables. He wrote Sweet Valley High books and a Scene! biography of Jennifer Love Hewitt. He posed for the covers of teen romance books, including Julie Taylor's aptly named *Falling for Ryan*. To keep his performing talents sharp, he bought a wolf costume and put on little shows on the sidewalk. He corrected college application essays. He wrote articles, too, "whatever I could hustle."

> **"Whatever you choose, make sure your moonlighting projects keep you focused on your mastodon—your main goal."**

He kept his friends abreast of his writing career. One, who worked for the International Federation of Competitive Eating (IFOCE), suggested that the wing- and hot dog–eating contests that this organization staged could be good story fodder. Nerz pitched a story to the *Village Voice* about a 400-pound conductor on the 7 train who had produced a hip-hop CD about his competitive eating career. The *Voice* bit. To interview the man, Nerz met him at Hooters for one of his training meals. He recorded the details as the man showed a rather disgusted waitress how he could pull all the meat off a chicken wing in one bite.

While the waitress was not impressed, the IFOCE was impressed with Nerz's reporting. They thought he "got" the concept. They approached him after the article appeared with a gig selling competitions to restaurants as a marketing technique. After he sold a few, they called and asked if he'd like to be the announcer at a meat pie–eating contest in Louisiana. He agreed to do it, in part for the free trip. Then he discovered that he had a talent for getting people excited about eating pies. He started announcing and judging contests regularly.

Suddenly, he was an entertainer. As for his writing career, Nerz soon realized that his time on the competitive eating circuit would make great material for a book. He pitched the topic to an agent, and they sold his tale, *Eat This Book: A Year of Gorging and Glory on the Competitive Eating Circuit,* to St. Martin's Press. As he wrote this satiating story, the plotting and dialogue techniques he learned writing Sweet Valley High books came in handy. Even the wolf costume has played a role. Late in the course of his competitive eating research, he participated in a contest dressed as a wolf, in part to create a character that could be useful in book publicity. All these grass and tree bark projects led Nerz to his mastodon—though, given what he knows about competitive eating, maybe he *could* eat more than one at a time.

FINDING BALANCE

So now you're chasing a mastodon and enjoying your fish and berries. You have a backup tree bark–munching plan that keeps you on the mastodon trail. Have you achieved caveman project nirvana in this Craig's List Economy?

Well, not quite. The good thing about building a career outside the grind is realizing that there's more to life than the grind. You can drag only one mastodon into your career cave at a time. But we have other caves in life beyond our careers. As I mentioned earlier in this chapter, Andrew Brooks of Maximum Balance labels these main areas of life Relationships, Financial, Personal, and Giving (with Career as the fifth). It's a useful framework. You might try dragging a mastodon or two home to these other caves as well. Brooks has been training for a marathon (Personal) and building a stronger relationship with his wife by taking dance lessons together (Relationships). Maybe you want to tackle buying a house (Financial) or building a solid after-school program for neighborhood kids (Giving).

None of this interferes with your career growth. Indeed, your neighbor on the after-school committee just might introduce you to an editor who's dying to hire a Scotch expert.

Pursuing personal mastodons can help you land your dream projects. While you're tracking game on the personal side, you may discover that your career mastodon is simply sitting there in the tar pit, smiling sheepishly and waiting for you.

GRINDHOPPING
GUIDELINE #5:

SEEK TO BE JUDGED *ON* RESULTS
Be better, and you've got it made

When she was two, children's book illustrator LeUyen (say "Le-win") Pham and her family fled the Communist takeover of Saigon. She remembers little of the trip to America from Vietnam; the voyage lodged in the shadowy parts of her mind like a dreamed adventure. Two decades later, though, Pham's ability to re-create dreamy scenes and adventures on a page let her flee a cushy job and strike out for a more rewarding career on her own.

Even when Pham was little, she toted a sketchbook everywhere. She drew people, objects, and scenes with her crayons. From the beginning, the joy and animation in her sketches caught people's eyes. She went to art school. When she finished, she landed a prestigious job at DreamWorks SKG studios. At 23, she was the youngest person on her team by far, and "the only girl," as she puts it. She worked with a lot of grizzled veterans of the animation industry. In the past, she says, animators had been forced into free agent lifestyles, since studios wouldn't hire them full-time. Then DreamWorks appeared on the scene. Suddenly studios had to compete for animation talent. These older men had spent their lives wandering, not necessarily by choice. They were happy to take stable jobs as they neared retirement. But their tales, told to impress young Pham in meetings, inspired a bad case of wanderlust in her.

So as she worked on *Prince of Egypt* and other films, she saved every penny. She paid off her student loans. And she conspired to find a way to set foot on every continent while she made a living from her art.

During her second year at DreamWorks, an old mentor helped Pham land a freelance book illustration project. She enjoyed laboring over the drawings and making the story she saw in her head appear on the page. She thought illustrating might be a good second career. So she quit her job, went on a travel binge across Asia, Africa, and Europe, and did a few small projects and a lot of sketchbook squiggles of elephants along the way.

At DreamWorks she'd been pulling in about $100,000 a year. Her first year freelancing, she made $12,000.

Fortunately, no one told Pham that that's typical for the children's book market. It's a rough field. The reason that many new titles in this genre are "written" by celebrities is that's it's difficult to stand out on the shelves any other way. It's also difficult to get on those shelves in the first place. Art directors at publishing houses receive thousands of postcards from artists seeking work. One in a hundred might grab their attention.

But Pham interpreted her low take as evidence that she needed to focus, not as evidence that thousands of artists were competing for the same scarce projects. When she settled down in San Francisco after her worldwide whirl, she chose ten picture book editors that she really wanted to work with. She created a lovingly illustrated little handmade picture book for each. That way, looking at her bright colors and the lit, beguiling faces of her characters, editors could judge her on the exact kind of results she would produce for them. She wrapped each book in brown paper. She included a note saying that she would be in New York in a month, and she would love to meet with them.

Seven of the ten editors called and offered her manuscripts.

"I never asked, 'Is this the norm?'" Pham says. She simply flew to New York, met her editors, and got a foothold in the industry. She's since done the art for over a dozen books, including Phil Bildner's *Twenty-One Elephants*. This whimsical tale features a nineteenth-century girl whose father won't let her walk over the Brooklyn Bridge until P. T. Barnum parades his elephants across it. *Booklist* praised it, noting that the "Expressive, warm-hued paintings, featuring apple-cheeked characters, capture nineteenth century Brooklyn, as well as Hannah's bright-eyed enthusiasm for the 'metal monster.'" Pham's first solo effort, *Big Sister, Little Sister*, about her relationship with her much-loved older sibling, hit stores in the summer of 2005.

Pham happily shares the picture book gimmick that she used to hook editors with the art students that she teaches on occasion. But there's a catch to being judged on results: you have to deliver them, too. "I've had publishers call me saying, 'Did you suggest that a student do this? The work is awful,'" she says. "It reinforces to me that these are just gimmicks to get you going. If you don't have the strength in your work to hold it up, you won't get anywhere."

If you do, on the other hand, there's no metal monster that you and your elephants can't parade across.

FLOUTING THE FACE-TIME CULTURE

LeUyen Pham wanted to be judged on results. All Grindhoppers do.

When you are young and striking out on your own, you can't win work based on your decades of experience in the industry or your long relationships with influential people. You can't point to your years spent paying your dues in a company hierarchy and say that you deserve the work.

You have to show what you can do and seek to be rewarded based on the performance that you deliver.

Personally, I think that's the fairest way to judge people. When you judge people on results, things like gender and race don't matter so much. Neither does age. You waste less time, because face time and politics become less important.

Most executives talk a good game about judging people this way. A 2005 Families and Work Institute survey found that 72 percent of workers said that supervisors at their companies were encouraged to assess performance by what people accomplished, not by face time.

However, only 31 percent of respondents said that management rewarded those who supported flexible arrangements. In business, money talks. What it's saying here is that whatever the official politically correct policies may be, executives still like having an office full

> **When you are young and striking out on your own, you can't win work based on your decades of experience in the industry or your long relationships with influential people. You can't point to your years spent paying your dues in a company hierarchy and say that you deserve the work. You have to show what you can do and seek to be rewarded based on the performance that you deliver.**

of people to "manage." Although 29 percent of employees in another Families and Work Institute survey freely admitted that they spent a lot of time doing work that they considered wasteful, in many companies, showing up early and staying late is still considered the red badge of courage. You score points by complaining in the cafeteria that you have *so* much work to do. You compare how many hours you had to work over the weekend. You whisper disparaging things about any coworker seen leaving before 5 p.m. You assume that working long hours means that you're important—not that you're slow.

I call this the face-time culture. It's a widespread phenomenon. A 2005 *Harvard Business Review* study by Sylvia Ann Hewlett and Carolyn Buck Luce found that 39 percent of professional women reported resistance to the idea of telecommuting in their workplaces. About a quarter to a third reported that coworkers and management attached a stigma to other practices like flextime and job sharing. The face-time culture's tentacles squeeze tighter when the labor market is weaker. A July 2005 report from the Department of Labor found that the number of Americans working flexible schedules fell from 29 million in May of 2001, as the dot-com boom was ending, to 27.4 million in 2004. A 2005 Society for Human Resource Management survey found that while 64 percent of companies offered flextime arrangements in 2002, only 56 percent did so in 2005.

The trend does not bode well for turning the face-time culture into a results culture any time soon. Indeed, for all the talk about judging people on results, the June 2005 Hudson Highland Group survey I cited in "Know Where You're Going," Guideline 2, found that 60 percent of workers say that tenure, not performance, determines pay where they work. We still believe that the ticket to advancement is having the boss see you working more hours for more years. My husband brings home his McKinsey Staff Papers from time to time; no. 63 from Tsun-yan Hsieh on "The Zen of Organization" contains this story: "A new CEO decided to come into the office at 6 a.m. rather than 7:30 to read up on his company's industry. As the first person to arrive, he turned on the lights. Within about a week, he noticed that, upon his arrival, the lights were already on; within three weeks, the entire executive staff was showing up at 6 o'clock."

In the face-time culture, it doesn't matter that the new CEO was showing up early to be *alone*.

The face-time culture also doesn't care if you do your work more efficiently than other people. In few companies can you finish all your work for the day by 3 p.m. and walk out the front door without asking permission or making excuses. Sure, in theory you could be dreaming up new solutions to problems in the next two hours before others start drifting out the door. But if your boss would rather you sit at your desk playing solitaire than go home—because he owns your time—then you are not being judged on results.

I won't pretend that the face-time culture is all the fault of insecure or lazy managers, though. Many workers don't want to be judged on results. They like having top executives smile at them for being there first thing in the morning. They think someone with ten years experience should earn more than someone with two as a matter of principle. As Bruce Tulgan, author of *Winning the Talent Wars*, explains it, "Time is a great equalizer. People tend to think there is a basic fairness when everybody is rewarded by the same measure: The more hours (or years) you work, the more you get paid." Anyone can figure out how to work more time, after all. Actually boosting the bottom line is a hairier question. It's one that few people like to ask themselves. Today's Organization Men and Women still believe the promise that William H. Whyte spelled out 50 years ago: that their loyalty to a company should buy the company's loyalty to them, regardless of productivity. That's why outsourcing generates such fury. Anyone who thinks it's unfair to have to justify his pay versus that of someone in Bangalore who could do the same job for a quarter of the cost, by definition doesn't want to be judged on results. And why should he? Executives aren't always judged by results, either. A 2002 *Financial Times* investigation found that top management in the 25 biggest recent U.S. corporate collapses walked away with $3.3 billion in share sales, payoffs, and other rewards.

Grindhoppers, on the other hand, hope that people will judge them and pay them based on what they do. They don't mind having their results compared against those of someone in Bangalore. Book editors, after all, hire Pham for her drawing style. They pay her for a performance that they don't believe anyone else on the planet can deliver exactly as she can. I hate the phrase "Brand You," but if you wish to be judged on results, you'd better be distinctive, and you'd better be better than other people at what you do.

> **The young people I interviewed for this book all had a deep interest in quality. It's not just because they're over-achievers. Quality is one place where microenterprises can compete.**

Grindhoppers are.

The young people I interviewed for this book all had a deep interest in quality. It's not just because they're overachievers. Quality is one place where microenterprises can compete.

You can't compete on years of experience, size, or range of products, and you can't compete on reach into markets.

But you can certainly be better.

So Grindhoppers work to be better. The guys who run Oral Fixation Mints, whom I profiled at the beginning of this book, don't just rely on sleek tins to lure their customers. The ingredients in their mints cost several times what other candy companies spend per tin. The mints have a smooth mouth feel. They taste better than other breath mints.

A devotion to quality also shows through in "impossible" fields such as art, music, literature, fashion, or other creative enterprises. The Grindhoppers I interviewed in these fields all wanted to share a secret about quality for those starting out. It's one they wish they'd known, and one that would have made hopping out of the grind much easier.

The secret? If you're very, very good at what you do, and you have a level head about the business side, it's not impossible to make a living in these fields.

Sometimes it's not even all that tough.

Laurie Kaufmann developed her flair for accessories at about the same age that Pham picked up her crayons. She used to walk around her grandmother's house toting multiple purses. Now she walks around the offices of Lorelei Design, LLC, in New York City's garment district carrying multiple purses. When I visited, the storeroom was strewn with shiny leather hobos, shimmering clutches, and canvas totes, all waiting for Kaufmann's sales reps to take them to accessories shows around the country.

Kaufmann worked in public relations for Calvin Klein for a year after college, but she always knew that she wanted to make handbags. So she enrolled in the Fashion Institute of Technology's year-long program on accessory design. There she learned the importance of good materials and good construction. "For something like this, the product has to work," she says. Her bags are certainly cute and fun, but if you look more closely, you can't miss her attention to detail. A blue eelskin clutch sports a frame that stays open, wide as an eel's mouth, so that you can find your keys without dumping your wallet on the floor. The vertical details in the vertically placed strips of eelskin echo the clutch's vertical stitching. One of Kaufmann's earliest designs, one that garnered her attention from the Daily Candy Web site and *Us Weekly*, followed the 2003 trend of using ribbons. But instead of simply sticking ribbons on her "Paget bag," Kaufmann actually stitched the ribbons into the bag's sides to hold the gathered fabric in place.

She took the Paget and a few other samples to Los Angeles soon after she launched her line. She and a friend walked into stores and showed the owners both the goods and the *US Weekly* and Daily Candy articles about them. Yes, these were carefully chosen high-end boutiques where a decision maker was likely to be on hand. But that paid off. Most looked. Most bought. "You can walk in cold, and they will order," Kaufmann says. "It blew my mind." She asked to be judged on results and, with the eye-catching results in hand, she landed retail account after retail account.

She worked out of her studio apartment at first. Around her various trunk shows, this meant piles of bags stacked on her floor. This also meant that store buyers stopping by Lorelei "headquarters" learned that they might have to sit on her bed to conduct a meeting. She'd bluff—"we're between leases"—but when the buyers looked at the bags, they didn't care. "Everyone who came, bought," she says. (You can see her line at Henri Bendel and on Eva Longoria's arms in the occasional episode of *Desperate Housewives*.)

Kaufmann has had a bit of an advantage—she's in a good field for Grindhoppers. In fashion, people want to discover new things that no one else knows about. It doesn't hurt to be young. Fashion is always about youth. Indeed, the question almost becomes how to maintain that fresh, youthful vibe when you reach the ripe age of 30.

IMPROVING QUALITY

You need a lot of innate talent to succeed in creative fields like fashion and the arts. I don't buy the line that success is 10 percent inspiration and 90 percent perspiration. If you don't have a big set of lungs, a pleasing vocal tone, and an outsized personality that draws people's eyes to you onstage, you are not going to make it as an opera singer. Even if you do sweat a lot. Sorry.

However, I will say that talent is only about 60 percent of the equation. I once interviewed star pianist Lang Lang about his childhood in Shenyang, China. From the time he was a little boy, Lang Lang could feel the nuances of a piece where other children would just play the notes. But there are lots of talented child pianists—even in Shenyang. What led Lang Lang to play in Carnegie Hall is that he practiced every day for hours from the time he could first sit still on a piano bench. Even in the cold flat that he and his father shared when they moved to Beijing to further his studies, he would play into the night as his father cooked, cleaned, and lay in the bed to warm it for him.

Lang Lang practiced all those hours because he knew that when you seek to be judged on results, you have to constantly improve your product. That's the bad news. The good news is that it's easy to get better if you are doing what you love. When you do what you love, you naturally spend your time thinking about it. You brainstorm new ideas or interpretations, and you solve problems while you're waiting in line at the grocery store. You find the process fun. This is one of the reasons I knew I should be a writer, not a pianist like Lang Lang. I studied the instrument as a kid, but my teachers had to shame me into practicing. Even so, I seldom played for more than an hour a day. But I wrote sonnets in the margins of school notebooks and scribbled furtively in my journals every night.

Here's how you can improve your craft:

- ⋯⋮ **Play with it.** When you love something, you experiment in ways that no one can see. Artists carry sketchbooks with them everywhere. Composers dabble with different chords and instrumental combinations. Handbag designers surround themselves with fabric scraps. In these play spaces, you see what works and figure out different ways of presenting things.

⋯⋗ ***Do a lot of it.*** I understand why hiring managers value experience. Most people get better the more they do something. You can't speed up the number of years you've worked in a field. You can, however, speed up the effect of experience by producing more than other people.

LeUyen Pham teaches a graduate art class. On the first day, she spreads out all the work she's done in the last six months for the class to see. With some artists, that would be one painting. For Pham, it could be two books, several fine art pieces, and a host of sketches. Let people be shocked at your level of output.

> **"Most people get better the more they do something. You can't speed up the number of years you've worked in a field. You can, however, speed up the effect of experience by producing more than other people."**

In theory, too much quantity might reduce quality, but most people are inefficient. Cranking out more than the average person doesn't mean that the quality will be less than that of the average person's work.

⋯⋗ ***See how other people are doing it.*** Are you a composer? Attend every world premiere you can find to see what arrangements are catching audiences' ears. Handbag designers should scope out other designers' trunk shows. Writers entering contests should read the entries that won the year before. Of course, you should never copy someone else's work, but I'm always amazed at how many creative types feel that they shouldn't be influenced by what else is out there. Nonsense. Smart artists take inspiration from anything they can find.

> **Learn from criticism of it.** In Pham's field of children's books, this can be especially harsh. If a kid gets bored with your story, she'll toss it aside. She doesn't care about your feelings. But Pham takes children's opinions seriously. "When a kid says 'Mommy, I want this book,' it's better than the *New York Times* book review," she says. Making a living in a creative field requires remembering that someone is consuming your creativity on the other end. I'm not saying that you should paint only in colors that match the average American's living room sofa. But there's a certain bias in the arts toward stories of artists who defied all the critics, were hated by the public, lived as misunderstood misfits, and starved as a result. After their deaths, though, they were recognized as geniuses. That's fine if you want to bet on that. But this is a book about building a career, not building up stacks of self-published novels in your garage. So show your work to people whom you respect and who will be brutally honest. Identify your target market and ask a few members to comment on whether they'd buy your work or push friends to do so. Some criticism is worthwhile and some isn't. But you should know the general trend, so that you can react if you wish.

> "In theory, too much quantity might reduce quality, but most people are inefficient. Cranking out more than the average person doesn't mean that the quality will be less than that of the average person's work."

HELPING THE NEEDY

Being judged on results is easier in artistic or product fields. I can taste Oral Fixation's Sugar Free Tibet mints. I can marvel at Pham's illustrations or covet Kaufmann's eelskin clutch. But many Grindhoppers enter spheres that are defined more by services or relationships. These tend to be low-cost businesses, so they're attractive options for young people. But unlike fashion, they're areas where there's no benefit in being new. Experience matters more to clients, and sometimes there's a justified fear of untested folks. I'm not sure I'd want a hip accountant who approached my taxes in a fresh, undiscovered way.

So how can you seek to be judged on results in these fields?

The Grindhoppers I interviewed had suggestions for overcoming these barriers. You can narrow your pitch to focus on an area where youth is an asset, so that people will be more willing to judge you on what you can do. A big company won't necessarily be interested in the comprehensive marketing campaign you could design for one of its products. But the executives might not know that advertising in podcasts could link their company with young people who skip TV ads with their TiVos. They certainly wouldn't know which podcasts to sponsor, nor would they have the technology on hand to deliver and track ads in multiple podcasts. Greg Galant, an entrepreneur in his 20s, founded the company RadioTail to help companies answer those exact questions and to provide those exact services.

You can also create a result that your clients can judge. I'm not suggesting that you work for free, but you can do things on spec at first. Rather than pitch your software-building services to a company and ask for a bid, you create a prototype of the software you think the company needs and let the decision maker play with it. This requires more of an up-front investment from you, but it takes the risk out of the decision for your client. When there's less risk, she's more inclined to say yes.

What these suggestions have in common is asking two questions:

1 **"What needs do my clients have?"**

2 **"How can I show them that I am the right person to meet those needs?"**

These are questions that require some digging. Meeting surface needs is less compelling than meeting deeper ones.

Gordon Smith and David Oblath did that kind of digging when they founded New York City–based Tutor Associates a few years ago. They knew that test preparation and academic tutoring were growing fields that didn't require a lot of start-up capital. Since most young people who graduate from good colleges seem qualified to go into the business, though, it was less clear how Smith and Oblath could attract families to them, specifically. After all, families could just pay the neighbor's brainy daughter to help instead.

So they asked why affluent Manhattan parents sought out tutoring. The obvious answer would be for their kids to get As and get into good colleges.

The less obvious answer, though, is that parents want less stress. They are busy. They love their children, and they want to help with their children's homework. But sometimes they don't know the subjects well, and sometimes they don't have the time and energy to manage both their own jobs and multiple children's academic lives. Sometimes children are organizationally challenged. That's where Tutor Associates comes in.

Tutor Associates can't promise that its clients' children will get straight As or get into good colleges. But it can deliver on reducing parental stress from the first phone call. The company can promise to provide a well-matched tutor without the parent's needing to call around. It can work with the family's schedule; Tutor Associates even opens an office in the Hamptons during the summer, since that's where many of its client families vacation. The company can send someone to work one-on-one with the child in the family's home during the school year. It can stress its carefully cultivated relationships with New York's top prep schools and, more importantly, its familiarity with those schools' schedules. Parents come away assured that their child will not announce at 10 p.m. the night before a major project is due that he just remembered the project. The kid's tutor will have known about the project for weeks.

Recognizing that deeper need helps Tutor Associates hold onto clients longer. If the company sold parents solely on getting their children into top colleges, parents would hire Tutor Associates tutors only for a child's junior and senior years of high school. As it is, parents hire the company for one child who needs help, then continue to use its services for the kid's younger brothers and sisters, and then refer the neighbors. That, in turn, means that Tutor Associates doesn't need to spend scarce capital on advertising.

Satisfying a deeper need gives you results that can compensate for a lack of experience. People don't choose cattle driving as an activity at Arizona resorts because herding large, smelly cows is fun. They do it to touch that lost part of childhood when they dreamed of being free-roaming cowboys. We don't hire closet organizers to alphabetize our shoes by designer. We hire them to make us feel more in control of our lives. So use that psychology class you took in college to figure out the wish your clients dare not speak.

OVERPROMISE AND OVERDELIVER

Once you've figured out that need, you need to deliver the results. If you read business books, you know about the importance of managing expectations. A disappointed client is less likely to rehire you than someone who gets better results than he bargained for. So the conventional wisdom is that you should underpromise and overdeliver.

That's fine if you're a 7,000-employee consulting firm with a 30-year track record. But what if you're trying to sell the relationships and industry knowledge of 20-something you?

You cannot afford to underpromise, as your potential clients are already worried that you'll underdeliver.

So you have to overpromise and overdeliver.

Ron Shah, head of the private equity firm Jina Ventures, discovered this both in his first job hunt out of college and when he started his company. After graduating from George Washington University, he struggled to find a full-time position. He finally got an interview with a venture capital firm and landed a five-minute meeting with the managing partner while he was there. The conversation didn't go well. The man was starting to say, "We'll get back to you," when Shah told him, dead straight, that he knew he had a good eye for the big picture of business. He knew he could put together the pieces of a company's story to see if it was a good investment. The man must have wondered how on earth a kid could be so sure of that, but he decided what the heck. Might as well let him try. Shah was given two weeks. If the office decided they liked him after two weeks, he could have a job. If not, they'd go their separate ways.

Shah stayed there for a year, rising fast through the ranks and vacuuming up every aspect of the business. Then he went to a hedge fund for a bit and learned about private equity and various financial instruments. Then he enrolled in an MBA program and figured that if he wanted to start a business, that was the time. So he founded Jina Ventures. Named after the ancient Sanskrit word for "conqueror of obstacles," this private equity firm has a business plan that calls for matching small- and midsized firms with funding opportunities and deals.

I've listed business ideas in other parts of this book that are Grindhopper-friendly. Just so you know, this one isn't.

First, you have to know the people who make decisions at the midsized companies and convince them that you can deliver the big bucks for them. Then you have to convince bigwigs at even bigger companies that you have discovered an incredible deal that they've got to see. People spend a lifetime in corporate America building up these kinds of connections. A 20-something man does not have these connections unless his father's name is Icahn.

Nonetheless, Shah, "conqueror of obstacles," was undeterred. "Everyone has an ear for a good deal," he told me. "If you have a good deal, it doesn't matter who you are."

> **When you let yourself be judged on big results, and then you deliver them, you wow the people you work with. When you lack experience, that's the easiest way to get ahead quickly, no matter what field you're in.**

With that in mind, he hunted for his first client. Someone a friend went to high school with knew the CEO of a well-positioned company with about $25 million in annual revenue. Shah got his meeting. He researched every aspect of the company, then told the CEO that he would get him a meeting with anyone he wanted.

Now, Shah knew a bit about business, but he did not know Barry Diller, the head of IAC/InterActiveCorp, which owns the Home Shopping Network, among other things. That was an issue, because the client wanted a meeting with Diller. No matter. Shah said he'd get him a meeting.

He composed a tight, compelling e-mail on why Diller had to meet this team. He knew that Diller's e-mail address had to be something at InterActiveCorp's domain name. So he sent e-mails to every version of Barry Diller (bdiller@, barry_diller@, barry.diller@, and so on) that he could think of.

One of them got through. A few days later, Diller's assistant called and said that the mogul had read the e-mail. He was intrigued. They got the meeting after all.

When you let yourself be judged on big results, and then you deliver them, you wow the people you work with. When you lack experience, that's the easiest way to get ahead quickly, no matter what field you're in.

There's a certain talent to this in relationship-based fields. Shah makes you feel comfortable. He's self-effacing, smiles a lot, and looks for ways to establish connections and be helpful. When I met him at his office in December of 2005, I gave him my business card. Instead of putting it away, Shah studied it, looked at my "office" address, and mentioned that he'd lived in the same apartment building briefly a few years ago, thus establishing an almost neigh-borly bond (though with 800 units on 57 floors, that's less of a coincidence than it sounds like). Within a few days, I had a lovely Christmas card from him in my mailbox and an e-mail in my inbox with a list of other Grindhoppers I should call.

On occasion, I've attempted to be thoughtful and helpful like this. I usually bungle the gesture somehow. My brain doesn't work that way.

But, like playing the piano, wowing people is also a skill. It means meeting deadlines, anticipating the next problem or question, and having an answer ready. It means doing your research and paying attention to small details. Shah created a signature file for the Barry Diller e-mail in the same style that he'd seen on e-mails from other deal-making firms. Not many people would have kept and studied random e-mails to discern such a pattern, but Shah knew that getting a meeting with Diller was chancy enough. If he had to overdeliver, he could leave nothing that he could control to chance. He didn't.

Now, over the years, he's discovered another happy Grindhopping truth: if you wow enough of the right people, you're set.

You'll never have to hustle for work again.

GRINDHOPPING
GUIDELINE #6:

EVERYTHING IS NEGOTIABLE
**From money to work-life balance,
don't believe "that's just the way it is"**

Whalen you hop out of the grind, you trade security for freedom. That can be a scary thing to do. The upside, of course, is that few of the old career rules apply. You can negotiate any new rules you desire. For people who don't like silly rules that other people dream up, that is a pulse-quickening prospect.

You do not have to settle for seeing your salary rise in 5 to 10 percent increments. There's no reason it can't double from year to year. If you feel that you should be making $100,000 a year by age 25, you can try to bag enough projects to bring in six figures. Good luck doing that in a corporation that hires entry-level employees at somewhere around the average 2006 starting salary for liberal arts majors of $30,958.

If you'd like to wear a certain style of clothes, fine. If you like to listen to music while you work, great. If you want to structure your business and your days around some inviolable commitment—like not waking up before 9 a.m.—you can do so. You can take on job responsibilities whenever you want to try them. Few people at big companies can decide if the firm will take on a major project unless they've been there a few years or run the place. Strike out on your own, though, and you'll be choosing your first projects before lunch. Whatever you can negotiate, you can have.

Of course, all this negotiation can frazzle your nerves. It's not necessarily fun to be constantly asking for things. Lots of people hate it. One of the reasons so many Americans bought cars when manufacturers offered the "employee pricing" incentive during the summer of 2005 is that people like to know that they're getting a fair deal without the haggling.

Women in particular, according to Linda Babcock and Sara Laschever's book *Women Don't Ask*, are likely to compare negotiating to going to the dentist.

I understand the dread it inspires. You think it will be painful and unpleasant. But if you read up a bit on what's happening and put yourself in the chair to face the situation, you'll discover it's not so bad. You'll feel silly for thinking otherwise.

I'm talking about going to the dentist. Negotiating actually makes my teeth hurt.

The problem, I've realized, is that I love what I do. I'm still tickled pink that people pay me to write. If I hated my job, I'd want people to pay through the teeth.

> **"Asking people to pay through the teeth for something you love so much that you'd do it for free is a hard thing to get your jaws around. But it's necessary."**

Asking people to pay through the teeth for something you love so much that you'd do it for free is a hard thing to get your jaws around.

But it's necessary.

We have to eat, or pay the mortgage, or feed a Banana Republic shopping habit, or whatever your particular need happens to be.

People who negotiate get more money and more of what they want. Some people actually think less of you if you don't negotiate or don't keep your rates high enough to show your professionalism.

So how do you do that, particularly if you're the youngest person at the negotiating table? I went to a pro for advice.

Susan Devenyi started her career as a lawyer on Wall Street. She loved the work, particularly training and mentoring her colleagues, but eventually she burned out on the hours. For years, she had taught negotiation classes on the side. "People were telling me this should be a business," she says. So she quit her job and started The Negotiation Company, which conducts seminars for individuals and groups on getting the right deal. Here are her tips for young negotiators:

> **People who negotiate get more money and more of what they want. Some people actually think *less* of you if you don't negotiate or don't keep your rates high enough to show your professionalism.**

····> *Do your homework.* What do the people across the table from you need and want? What do other people charge for such a service? What have companies or people like this paid before? As both parties need to feel like they've won something, what value does the other person get out of you that justifies your rates? Work your network until you know the numbers for your industry. See Grindhopping Guideline 7 for tips on building a network. Whatever you do, don't aim too low. Underselling yourself will make you seem inexperienced. While aiming too high makes you seem naïve, young people—and young women in particular—don't err on this side too often.

····> *Be yourself, but maybe not your craziest self.* Soft factors help make people comfortable. If your clients are big on nice stationery in leather folders, get some stationery in a leather folder. I know that forgoing meaningless status symbols and uncomfortable clothing is a big appeal of hopping out of the grind, but you can still show some personality in a suit, if you're expected to wear one. Men can wear a colorful shirt and a distinctive watch; women can try an interesting blouse and bohemian jewelry instead of a whole bohemian outfit. In more creative fields, you can stretch the boundaries. Tony Ruth worked as a freelance illustration consultant before he cofounded consumer research firm Vessel Ideation. "For a while there I had blue hair and showed up to every meeting on my bike, but nobody cared because that wasn't inconsistent with anyone's notion of being a young, urban-dwelling digital artist," he says. Still, you should be aware of the image you're projecting. Wearing last year's hemlines shows a group of fashion editors that you don't know your stuff.

⋯⋗ ***Have an answer for why your youth is an asset.*** It's the elephant in the room. "A lot of managers may be skeptical about young talent," says Ruth, "but if you can be both professional and youthful at the same time, they know there's a huge value to it." We live in a youth-oriented culture. You know that your clients need you to figure out what the kids are doing these days.

⋯⋗ ***Practice beforehand.*** Buy a friend a drink in exchange for having her role-play your client or vendor. Bonus points if your friend is actually in the same industry as your client or vendor. Figure out what questions will trip you up, and how it sounds to actually say the numbers or conditions you want. You don't want to flinch or squirm when you say them for real.

⋯⋗ ***Don't make your statements sound like questions.*** It makes you sound insecure? And whiny, like this? The people across the table already know you're young. They don't need to think you're inexperienced and unsure of what you're doing, too.

A lot of the negotiation books out there have more suggestions. They point out that if the money won't budge, you can negotiate for other things. While ideas like job titles, increased vacation days, and flextime have little meaning for Grindhoppers, you can negotiate deadlines. If the client insists on paying $3,000, not $4,000, then he can have the project in two weeks, not one. You can negotiate for copyrights, long-term work agreements (you'll do this project for less if you're guaranteed two others this year), or introductions or recommendations to other clients. You can ask for testimonials that you can use in advertising, fewer site visits, dedicated onsite office space, a company e-mail address, or whatever you want.

I'll add two more of my own negotiation suggestions that took me longer to learn than I would have liked. The first is that it's okay to say no. If a project doesn't sound appealing to you, and you don't think the money is right, don't waste your time on it. That's why it's good to have six months worth of expenses in the bank. When you have that, you never get so desperate for work that you take projects that turn work into a dues-paying grind. If simply saying no bothers you, recommend someone else for the project, or offer to work your network to find someone whose "skills better match the opportunity."

The second is for people who can't stand hardball negotiating. If the project is right, but the money isn't, smile sweetly and say, "Oh, Sue, I'd so like to work with you. Is this the best you can do?" Then shut up and wait. Often, it isn't. You'll be glad you asked.

NEGOTIATING THE CAREER TRACK

Those are the basic negotiating techniques that Grindhoppers need to master. If you're the sort of person who's looking to build a career without paying your dues, though, my guess is that you're already pretty comfortable with asking for what you want in the money and perks department. So I won't dwell on that. To Grindhoppers, the "everything is negotiable" creed isn't just about money, anyway. It also means challenging widely held assumptions about the way the real world works. Among them:

1 **There are no short cuts to getting promoted.**
2 **Working for an established company is the best way to learn a craft.**
3 **Switching careers is tough.**
4 **You can't do good and make money at the same time.**
5 **If you hop out of the grind, good luck hopping back in to a position of authority.**
6 **Flexibility and work-life balance are only for people who've earned them with face time.**

Most of this book features the stories of people in their 20s and early 30s. For this chapter, I needed the perspective of people who'd been in the working world a bit longer. I wanted to know if young people could use free agency to get where they wanted in life.

The answer? Sure. But most of us don't really believe it. "Young people are risk averse. They believe in careers," one man who hopped out of the grind in his 20s, some 40 years ago, told me. They have yet to experience the frustration of being passed over for promotions for political, not performance, reasons. They don't realize that they can spend their whole lives struggling up the corporate ladder and still not hit the top rung because the guy on the top rung isn't retiring. Looking forward, they figure they're better off paying their dues now because they want the rewards of a big, steady paycheck when they start families of their own. They worry that they won't be able to hop back into the grind if they hop out. Or maybe their dream job is in a regimented career track, such as the law or education, or even the nonprofit world. And yes, the corporate world does have some perks, particularly when you're at the top of the heap.

> **While some companies cherish the idea that the guy who starts out in the mailroom can work his way up to being CEO, at many companies the talent pipeline is so broken that there's no clear path from the entry level to the top. This means that doing your own thing, while letting it be known that you could be wooed into the fold, is no more risky than starting at the bottom and working your way up.**

But "everything is negotiable" means everything is negotiable. Well, almost everything. While I've met doctors who started their own practices around age 30, I haven't come across anyone who's gotten to perform surgery without going to medical school. Some dues paying is okay. Everything else is pretty much up for grabs.

Indeed, while some companies cherish the idea that the guy who starts out in the mailroom can work his way up to being CEO, at many companies the talent pipeline is so broken that there's no clear path from the entry level to the top. This means that doing your own thing, while letting it be known that you could be wooed into the fold, is no more risky than starting at the bottom and working your way up.

Here's how several Grindhoppers have negotiated their own versions of career truisms that other people assume are "just the way it is."

YES, THERE ARE SHORTCUTS

Gil Silberman started law school at the "relatively advanced" age of 28. He realized that reaching the upper end of the profession—being a partner at a major firm—would take three years of law school followed by a ten-year partnership track (eight years as an associate and two years as a junior contract partner). That would make him 41 by the time he reached an equity position at a firm, and that would be only the beginning of a new climb. Partnership, the joke goes, is like a pie-eating contest. The prize? More pie.

So Silberman decided to take a different route. He started his own law firm right out of law school. He and his partners knew that they couldn't compete with the big firms on their own turf. So they did an end run around them.

"We specialized in doing what every lawyer wanted to do but didn't for some reason out of a sense of professional decorum," he says. That meant "things like acting like real people; thinking of the firm as a business rather than a profession; realizing the value of PR, marketing, and branding." They portrayed themselves as a different, more accessible kind of law firm. Since this was the late 1990s in San Francisco, they won the business of companies that wanted to tie themselves to the city's entrepreneurial vibe. The partners in Silberman's firm appeared on the cover of one law-oriented publication with the headline "Young, Hip, Cool, and Fun."

The clients kept coming in. "My firm was so hot that we got bought out by a major firm three years later and I was made a midlevel partner," Silberman says. Essentially, he earned 12 to 15 years seniority in 3. "The lesson I took is that you never get to the kitchen by coming in the front door."

That's a lesson that few people starting law school and dreaming of big firm partnerships consider. But it's one worth thinking about. Seniority systems are there if you wish to believe they're there. If you don't, well, everything is negotiable.

LEARNING WITHOUT PAYING YOUR DUES

Another career truism is that while paying your dues in the lower levels of a big company is a grind, you can't beat the paid training. We don't spring from the womb knowing all the best ways to serve legal clients, or how to run a billion-dollar corporation. Companies have seniority systems and ladders because all of us need time to learn the ropes.

The problem is that the dues-paying jobs at the bottom of many companies' ladders don't actually teach you a lot about those ropes. Or they make you spend so much time learning the ropes that good people leave the industry because really, if they see another rope, they're going to scream.

A few years ago, I cowrote a book on gifted education. The bright children I interviewed spoke of the frustration of being forced to spend a whole year learning algebra when they had mastered the concepts in six weeks. Some checked out mentally. Some learned the unfortunate lesson that curiosity only makes you miserable. Interviewing Grindhoppers, I've seen the same impatience in play.

The brightest, most ambitious young people learn their crafts faster than career tracks say they can. Some companies and some wonderful managers are happy to harness this energy. But others say the equivalent of "slow down, little one!"

> **The brightest, most ambitious young people learn their crafts faster than career tracks say they can. Some companies and some wonderful managers are happy to harness this energy. But others say the equivalent of 'slow down, little one!'**

The publishing industry is one of the worst offenders in this regard. If you want to work in magazines, conventional wisdom says, you need to start with an editorial assistant job at a major consumer title. Lots of industry bigwigs built their careers this way. Anna Wintour started as a fashion assistant in the early 1970s and is now the editor-in-chief of *Vogue*.

But as the ad dollars that finance staff positions flee to other media, the competition for editorial assistant publishing jobs has become so fierce that many would-be editors do low- or no-paying postgraduation internships before landing that first EA job. Then, as an EA, you earn $30,000 a year to answer the phones or empty outboxes. It will be years before you can climb to levels where you actually assign and edit major stories and thus get better at editing and planning a magazine. Some people don't want to spend that long working as a waiter on the side to afford the wardrobe that some of the more glamorous New York titles expect.

David Haskell didn't want to spend his twenties learning about magazines by answering someone's phones. So he decided to learn about the magazine industry by starting a magazine himself.

He was a graduate student at Cambridge University in 2001 when he and some friends started *Topic*, a magazine that *The Nation* later described as "a chocolate sampler for the mind." Since they were "broke from the very beginning," *Topic*'s editors had to look at their competitive strengths. They couldn't pay top dollar for top writers. They didn't think they could approach politics better than other magazines. They wanted something interesting that they—and their young, advertiser-desirable peers—would read.

So *Topic* followed the memoir trend and focused on first-person essays. Each issue covers one topic—for example, food or prison— through personal essays from people with experience in the area. Past contributors have included a convicted murderer, a Nobel laureate, a competitive eater, and a used-car salesman.

Haskell built the magazine from Great Britain and played up his outsider credentials as a way to meet people in the publishing industry. Eventually, he did decide to move himself and the magazine to New York. As the saying goes, if you can make it there, you'll make it anywhere.

It wasn't easy. He waited on tables to support himself. He edited business school application essays to make extra cash. Then again, so do many magazine editorial assistants. Haskell was waiting on tables while learning to run a magazine, doing everything from brainstorming issue concepts to assigning articles, choosing art, supervising layout, working with advertisers, drumming up money, landing subscribers, scoring magazine rack placement, and dealing with reader feedback. Each issue got easier. With a young, upscale readership, he attracted some A-list advertising. He got e-mails from people who were "just sort of stuck somewhere and want to be somewhere else." They volunteered their services. The design and copy got better with their expertise.

Haskell would like to have *Topic* win a National Magazine Award in the next few years. It's a possibility. Readers of the *Chicago Tribune* voted *Topic* the "14th best magazine in the nation," and *Topic* has won design awards.

Haskell is committed to staying with the publication for now to watch it grow. Eventually he might decide to try out the mainstream consumer magazine world. With *New Yorker* editor David Remnick calling *Topic* "terrific and beautifully done from start to finish," though, my guess is that Haskell won't have had to answer anyone's phone but his own to get his start in magazines. He'll have created his own training, and his own experience, without waiting for anyone else to deem him ready for it.

DEEP DABBLING

Once upon a time, a young person starting his working life could reasonably assume that he would stay at the same company for decades. Now, though, as more folks in the grind discover that the grind is not all it's cracked up to be, there's been a surging interest in switching not just jobs, but *careers*. A 2004 University of Phoenix survey of more than 6,000 adults found that 23 percent were unhappy with their careers and were considering a career switch. There's even a company, VocationVacations (profiled in the chapter on Grindhopping Guideline 1), that specializes in helping people dabble in different careers before taking the plunge.

Much of the career-change literature is of the hand-holding variety. That's because people assume that you'll have to go back to school, pay your dues again, lose income, or scramble to attain the authority you had before.

When you do your own thing, though, that's not necessarily the case.

"I'm no longer young," long-time Grindhopper Ed Miller said in an e-mail to me, "so perhaps I don't qualify for your research, but I managed to skip some aspects of dues paying in the journalism grind by starting my own small-town weekly newspaper (the *Harvard Post* in rural Harvard, Massachusetts) right out of college back in 1973."

Intrigued, I called him up to learn about this Grindhopping endeavor. The *Harvard Post*, it turned out, wasn't the only thing Miller had started over the past 30 years. The list also included a book publishing company, a teen magazine called *Highwire*, the nonprofit Opus 118 Harlem School of Music, and a consulting company, Great Pond, that works with nonprofits in the arts, education, and music. He'd also had an academic career as a teacher at Harvard University and elsewhere, without a PhD. In other words, he'd managed to hop over the grind in journalism, publishing, academia, and the nonprofit world. And he'd had a pretty good run of it in each sphere.

Miller learned the benefits of Grindhopping at a young age. His parents, both immigrants from Eastern Europe and members of the Communist Party, ran their own newspaper delivery business in Teaneck, New Jersey. While entrepreneurial Communists may seem like a contradiction in terms, the setup had its advantages. During the Red Scare in the 1950s, when other Communist Party members lost their jobs, the Millers kept delivering the *New York Times*, the *Newark Star-Ledger*, and their other papers unperturbed.

"I got the sense that you're better off staying somewhat outside the system," Miller says.

That bucking-the-system attitude, coupled with being "young, confused, and irresponsible," got him in trouble at times. He went to Harvard, but he flunked freshman expository writing. Then he flunked out entirely. He eventually came back and graduated with a degree in music, but he didn't have any particular musical aspirations beyond forming some sort of utopian commune where he'd play chamber music with friends. Hey, it was the early 1970s.

Instead of forming a commune, however, he and his wife moved to the small town of Harvard in central Massachusetts. People kept asking what he planned to do, so, reminiscing about his parents' newspaper business, he decided to start a newspaper. Thus the *Post* was born. After running the newspaper for several years, Miller decided to start a book publishing company called the Harvard Common Press. One of its books on a subject near to his heart, *How to Produce a Small Newspaper: A Guide for Independent Journalists*, became a minor classic. Because of Miller's experience with newspapers and publishing, he was approached shortly thereafter by another entrepreneur, who wanted him to help start a magazine for high school kids called *Highwire*.

The magazine lasted for only a few years, but it was extremely well edited, which did not escape the notice of Richard Marius, the legendary head of Harvard University's freshman expository writing program. He hired Miller to teach the same class that had tripped the young man up earlier. "I may be the only person who ever taught expository writing at Harvard who actually flunked it when I took it myself," Miller says. This was the beginning of his academic career.

The standard academic career ladder involves earning a PhD, then finding a tenure-track position at a college or university. Such positions are considered academic plums; once you achieve tenure, you can't be fired, you tend to earn more money, you get to devote more time to research, and people generally say that you've "made it."

Tenure-track jobs can involve a decades-long financial commitment from a university, though. Lifetime employment is disappearing in most other places, so it's not surprising that more universities are relying on what they call adjunct professors to keep costs down and introduce labor flexibility.

Adjunct professors are generally independent contractors. They teach classes for certain set amounts (say, $5,000 a section). Since adjunct professors generally have PhDs and would prefer tenure-track jobs, many see themselves as the academic equivalent of temps. They rage against universities' duplicity in cranking out PhDs on the one hand while hiring few tenure-track professors on the other. The Modern Language Association counted only 431 tenure-track English hires in 2001, compared with 977 English PhDs granted. One 1999 study found that only 53 percent of students who received English doctorates between 1983 and 1985 were tenured professors by 1995. A mere 8 percent were tenured professors at "Carnegie Research I institutions"—schools with their own major doctoral programs.

That's fine if everyone knows the odds. But 51 percent of these folks took nine or more years to finish their degrees; 95 percent took more than five. Young PhDs have plenty to complain about with the adjunct situation. I won't deny that.

But the increased use of adjunct professors does open up the possibility of teaching at great institutions to folks who don't want to follow the traditional academic route. "Schools don't necessarily publicize it in this day where rankings count for everything," Miller says. But "it's more possible to do that kind of thing without a PhD than most people assume." Academic researchers are not the only people with interesting things to teach students. Smart universities realize this.

Miller taught at Harvard for eight years. Marius encouraged him to design his own courses. He taught one on writing about music. He started taking classes in Harvard's Graduate School of Education on artistry in education. He kept playing chamber music. One musician he played with, a charismatic woman named Roberta Guaspari, told him that she taught children in East Harlem in New York City how to play classical violin. The kids were really good, she said, and he should come hear them. He did. He was duly impressed.

Then, in the midst of the city's early 1990s budget cuts, Guaspari's violin program landed on the chopping block. Miller thought they should form an organization to save it.

This was the beginning of his nonprofit career.

After that much experience at starting ventures, Miller didn't see any reason to work through an existing arts or education nonprofit in New York. Because of his journalism background, he recognized the value of good PR. He called the *New York Times* and local television programs and suggested that they do stories on Guaspari's kids. He requested, and got, pro bono legal help to become established as a 501(c)(3) nonprofit organization. He wrote every potential musical funding source in New York. Some rather famous people, from Isaac Stern to Itzhak Perlman, got involved. A benefit concert in Carnegie Hall that they organized raised $750,000 in a night. The Opus 118 Harlem School of Music was off to a great start. It was the stuff of movies (indeed, documentary film maker Allan Miller's work on Guaspari, called *Small Wonders*, was nominated for an Academy Award in 1996, and Meryl Streep starred in a fictional 1999 version of Guaspari's story called *Music of the Heart*). Having gotten the nonprofit bug, Miller started working with the Alliance for Childhood in Washington, DC, and started his own consulting company to help other nonprofits achieve their goals.

Through his different careers, Miller has maintained the same philosophy he learned while watching his Communist parents keep both their livelihoods and their beliefs. "Sometimes if you really want to get something done, you're better off starting your own thing instead of trying to work through existing channels," he says.

DOING GOOD AND DOING WELL

Many of us graduate from college hoping to change the world. Each year, students at over 100 colleges sign the "Graduation Pledge," in which they vow "to explore and take into account the social and environmental consequences of any job I consider" and to "try to improve these aspects of any organization for which I work."

For all we hope to do good works, though, we believe there's a trade-off. Either you go work for a company and earn big bucks so that you can make donations, or you go labor for saintly-low wages at a nonprofit that's saving humanity.

I've always thought that the conventional wisdom on this subject is too black and white. Plenty of companies don't pay well, and plenty of jobs high up the nonprofit ladder feature rather fat paychecks. According to Charity Navigator, Red Cross interim president Jack McGuire had a $416,010 salary in the fiscal year ending in June 2004. Reynold Levy, president of Lincoln Center for the Performing Arts, pulled in $577,500.

I have no problem with the heads of such big organizations earning big paychecks. I do have a problem with inefficiencies, however, and if the complaints I've heard from young people paying their dues in the nonprofit grind are to be believed, the bureaucracies of some big charities put for-profit companies to shame. The paper pushing and politics chase away good people. And some charities are so busy fundraising that they don't get around to doing much good. According to Charity Navigator, Hale House, the home for children set up by the famous Mother Clara Hale of Harlem, spends $1.33 in order to raise $1 for its programs. Maybe that's because donors are still sore about two executives stealing more than $700,000 from the organization a few years ago.

Some Grindhoppers respond to the inefficiencies and hazards of big nonprofits by founding their own. That's the approach Ed Miller took. But others decide that when you run a business the way you want, earning a profit doesn't mean that you can't do good at the same time.

> **" When you run a business the way you want, earning a profit doesn't mean that you can't do good at the same time. "**

"I would love to prove that there doesn't have to be a distinction between those two things," Hayden Hamilton tells me. "You can do both simultaneously."

Hamilton, an Oregon-based Grindhopper, started ProgressiveRx to provide low-cost imported drugs to people who don't have health insurance. He got the idea after several family members who had lost jobs asked him to purchase small quantities of drugs for them while he was visiting a friend in Asia. He was amazed at the price difference between drugs in the United States and drugs sold in other countries. He spent a few months doing due diligence, then filled his first order in May 2004. He never advertised (so no, he's not the guy spamming your inbox with Viagra ads), but word-of-mouth boosted sales by 600 percent in 2005.

You can disagree politically with Hamilton's business. He certainly operates on the margins of the law. People provide evidence of their prescriptions (such as a digital image). Then ProgressiveRx orders up to a 90-day supply of the drug through an international hospital chain that purchases its drugs from India. The FDA forbids organizations from importing drugs in most cases, though some states are experimenting with facilitating lower-priced imports from Canada and elsewhere. The FDA does allow individuals to import small quantities of drugs for their own use in certain circumstances, though such circumstances are supposed to be rare. In theory, imported drugs might not be as safe as drugs produced specifically for the American market. In reality, ProgressiveRx drugs were produced at FDA-approved factories in India, albeit not for the U.S. market. ProgressiveRx also does not sell scheduled drugs (e.g., easily abused drugs such as Vicodin) to avoid legal issues. But the drugs Hamilton does sell reach consumers for 80 percent off American retail prices—and he still makes a profit. The vast majority of his customers have no health insurance at all, and only 1 to 2 percent have prescription drug coverage of any kind. Many have told him that without ProgressiveRx, they would not be able to afford their drugs.

Hamilton pays himself an agreeable salary. Then he plows much of the rest of his profits into Progressive Health Worldwide, a healthcare delivery service he started recently. The service's first project is a mobile pediatric tuberculosis clinic in rural Karnataka, India. The clinic consists of a doctor, a nurse, and a Jeep. The team visits 50 pediatric TB patients in the area to deliver the children's antibiotics and to make sure they take them. By directly observing the therapy, the TB clinic's team can help to lower rates of drug resistance. Since many of these children are poor and malnourished as well, the doctor and nurse bring along fortified rice balls on their rounds. The extra protein and vitamins in the rice balls help the kids fight their infections, at a cost of 10 rupees, or about 25 cents, a day.

Plenty of big companies encourage volunteering, and plenty give big bucks to charity. But these acts are primarily recruiting, retention, and PR tools. There's nothing wrong with that. Public companies in particular need to stay focused on their profit margins. Since Hamilton runs his own show, though, he can focus on whatever he wants. He sees the TB clinic as part of his main business mission. "Progressive helps people afford their medications who otherwise wouldn't be able to," he says. This goes for both pediatric TB patients in India and people without health insurance in the United States. He also sees the clinic as a way of thanking the Indian community for helping him bring Indian-produced drugs to America. Both the drug business and the clinic have taught him that it's possible to be passionate about your work, something that he felt was missing during his first and only "real" job, a brief tenure at Ford Motor Company. There, people showed up because it was "pretty cushy," he says. "You can come in at 8:30, leave at 4, get a month's vacation, and it's nearly impossible to get fired."

Now, he comes to work because several thousand Americans and several dozen Indian kids need the drugs he's providing. It's a far more motivational alarm clock.

HOPPING BACK IN

One of the biggest misperceptions that young people have about striking out on their own is that once they do, they'll have a tough time reentering corporate America at a high level of pay and prestige. If you're worried about this, don't be.

Everything is negotiable to Grindhoppers, and that includes the ability to hop into and out of the grind as you see fit.

If you're worried about "gaps" on your résumé, then don't put yourself in a situation where you need a résumé. Simply tell some of your clients that you're interested in job opportunities. If you've been wowing them with your work, you're quite likely to be approached when there's an opening. Or they'll create a job for you.

> **Everything is negotiable to Grindhoppers, and that includes the ability to hop into and out of the grind as you see fit.**

That's what happened for Isabella Califano. Though she was

a championship rower in college, her résumé, she says, screams the message, "This girl cannot play in a team environment." She grew impatient in her first corporate job out of school. She wanted more work, but no one wanted to give it to her. So by the time she was 25, she left and started her own clothing line, Chickabiddy. She and a business partner designed and sold resort and active wear for six years. Then they realized they had different visions of where the company was going. Eventually, Califano's partner bought her out, and they went their separate ways.

Even before she left Chickabiddy, though, Califano started doing freelance projects for other companies. She worked with a talent agency to find gigs that could leverage her retail and marketing skills. She worked for a Web site that sold high-end men's products, among other places. Then she got a call from Pottery Barn Kids. The company needed help designing a brand revitalization program. Califano threw herself into the work. Using her expertise from having managed a business, she pulled together information from across functions. She turned the project around quickly. Her manager presented the results and got the project approved by Williams-Sonoma's leaders. This, not surprisingly, endeared Califano to everyone involved.

So "they bent over backwards to make a position for me," she says. Now, with the title of design manager, she leads the team that decides the mood and message of Pottery Barn Kids stores.

She feels fortunate that she found a company that didn't demand a specific career track; a coworker actually worked as a professional dancer for ten years before coming onboard. But in general, "if your work is really good, people might overlook a bizarre path," she says. Indeed, running Chickabiddy turned out to be good training for navigating a corporate environment. "Running a business is so humbling that I'm more attuned to how I work with people," she says. "I'm substantially more respectful of business. I had a hot head earlier."

A NEW MOMMY TRACK

All these new takes on career truisms are exciting. But the most revolutionary way in which Grindhoppers are rewriting the "normal" career rules is by challenging the assumptions that people hold on the vexing topic of work-life balance.

The blogosphere and the pundits like to work themselves into a good howl on this topic from time to time. In 2002, Sylvia Ann Hewlett's book, *Creating a Life*, ignited a fire with her finding that 49 percent of executive women earning over $100,000 a year were childless at age 40 (and hence would probably stay in that state). Former Harvard President Larry Summers fanned the flames with his statements in early 2005 that the most prestigious jobs in academia and business require complete devotion to work during your younger years, and hence women wouldn't appear at the top of these professions unless they made certain trade-offs. Jack Welch notes in *Winning* that, "The truth is, your boss wants 150 percent of you and, if you are good enough, he will do almost anything to get it, even if your family wants 150 percent too." This either/or setup contributes to both the low rate of childbearing among high-earning women and the rise in the number of stay-at-home moms from 4.5 million in 1994 to 5.4 million in 2003. With all the rhetoric, it just seems too tough to do both. As Yale student Cynthia Liu told the *New York Times* in a September 2005 article about elite college women's life plans, "My mother's always told me you can't be the best career woman and the best mother at the same time. . . . You always have to choose one over the other."

But remember, trade-offs are inevitable only when you have the mindset that someone else should be your boss. When you are the boss, you don't have to compromise if you don't choose to.

Young Grindhopping moms refuse to play in the chit system where face time earns flexibility. They wager that they can do better than the male model of work that says that hierarchies, meetings, and spending 70 hours a week away from your loved ones is living. They're carving their own paths that blend work and family.

The number of women-owned businesses rose 17 percent from 1997 to 2004, according to the Center for Women's Business Research, vs. 9 percent for all firms.

Dorit Zeevi-Farrington is one such business-owning mom. After serving as an officer in the Israeli Defense Forces, she moved to New York, earned her MBA, then did a stint in the grind. She excelled at it, climbing the ladder of a Wall Street trading firm to the first vice president level. She logged long hours. She traveled the world. She earned "close to seven figures."

Then in 2001 she had a baby. That changed everything.

"I couldn't see a nanny raising my daughter," she says. Within a year of returning from maternity leave, she volunteered for the next round of layoffs. Her superiors protested, but she insisted, and soon Zeevi-Farrington joined the ranks of high-achieving moms opting out of the traditional workforce.

This is the point in the story where the howling from the chattering classes begins. Why couldn't Zeevi-Farrington's company have had a better flextime policy or onsite child care? Why didn't she stick it out to strike a blow for the sisterhood? Or, from the traditionalists, see, bright women know they shouldn't work when their kids are little!

> **"Young Grindhopping moms refuse to play in the chit system where face time earns flexibility. They wager that they can do better than the male model of work that says that hierarchies, meetings, and spending 70 hours a week away from your loved ones is living. They're carving their own paths that blend work and family."**

But both traditionalists and traditional feminists miss what's happening on the front lines. Zeevi-Farrington's story doesn't stop with her severance check. She took the money and ordered a custom-designed 62-foot yacht, the *Noa Danielle*. She decorated it like Jay Gatsby's sitting room. Now Manhattan Steamboat Company, her family business, whisks revelers around New York's harbors. With clients including IBM and Novartis, Manhattan Steamboat is not yet clearing "close to seven figures," but it's getting there, with Zeevi-Farrington's daughter often playing onboard.

In other words, she has it all.

I'll admit that Zeevi-Farrington's previous high paychecks, her years of experience, and her generous severance package made hopping out of the grind a lot easier than it is for many Grindhoppers (though I wouldn't call walking away from a near $1 million paycheck easy, either).

But moms who are looking to hop out of the grind need not choose such capital-intensive businesses. After hearing Zeevi-Farrington's story, I interviewed a number of other mom entrepreneurs in their 20s and 30s who started less expensive businesses or freelancing ventures when they had less experience than our Wall

Street–turned-yachting heroine. Mompreneurs, like moms, run the gamut. But all share the belief that you can achieve work-life balance if you want to by creating your own rules. Everything is negotiable. If you know you can be superproductive and run a business in the four hours your baby-sitter has your two toddlers every day, or the time your kids are in school or with their dad, fine. If you want your toddlers to be your sidekicks sometimes, that's cool, too.

Mompreneur Chris McCurry of Blowing Rock, North Carolina, takes the latter approach. A former holistic nurse, she had always worked part-time with her husband on Highland Craftsmen, their environmentally friendly wood products company. When they started a family in 2003, she joined the venture full-time. She promptly doubled Highland Craftsmen's business. Unlike most construction company higher-ups, though, McCurry eats breakfast, lunch, and dinner with her son. The little guy spends some time with a baby-sitter and some time in the office or forest with mom trying to "help."

"I feel extraordinarily lucky," she told me. It beats a cubicle any day.

GRINDHOPPING
GUIDELINE #7:

CULTIVATE A NETWORK *AND* A NIMBLE MIND
Learn how to learn on the job

A h, networking. I feel funny writing a chapter on this topic because I am quite bad at networking in the conventional sense. For starters, I'm shy. You wouldn't think that someone whose profession involves calling people up and asking nosy questions would be shy, but I am. I do what I have to, professionally. But there have been days when I've interviewed half a dozen people and then I fight with my husband over which one of us has to make a dinner reservation because I don't want to cold-call a stranger.

Second, I'm disorganized. My "Rolodex" is a stack of business cards piled on top of the box that holds my business cards, which is sitting under some ponytail holders and three receipts from Kinko's that I've yet to file anywhere. That's because my desk features no filing system apart from having drawers. I don't file e-mails. One of my inboxes is searchable, so that helps me keep track of contact info. That's a good thing, because I don't have an address book. The other inbox isn't searchable, or else the search function is broken. I can't figure it out. I once scrolled through a year of e-mails to find someone's contact information, because I remembered that the person had e-mailed last March.

Some people might be embarrassed by these revelations. The lack of an address book *is* embarrassing. But for me, knowing these truths about myself made reading through recent best-selling networking books, such as Keith Ferrazzi's *Never Eat Alone*, a frustrating experience.

The books suggest things that are impossible. Imitate Bill Clinton's ability to remember names! Sure. While I'm at it, I'm also going to imitate Michael Jordan's jump shot.

They talk a lot about soft selling and near-military-style organization techniques. Jeffrey Meshel's new book on networking, *One Phone Call Away*, focuses on how he built his 5,000-name database of contacts. His system includes searchable notes about what each person is looking for or has to offer. That way, if someone says he's looking to hire an accountant with expertise in California real estate transactions, Meshel can search and find three such accountants. He also sends e-mails to all 5,000 of his contacts on occasion. One time, he sent an e-mail detailing a friend's offer to appraise or repair jewelry in exchange for a contribution to a charity that the man liked. According to the book, techniques like this have had the benefit of getting Meshel's name in front of 5,000 people without selling them anything. Many people call to talk business as a result.

If I sent a mass e-mail, I'd probably get a lot of people calling me, too. But that's because they would be wondering if someone had hacked my e-mail account and miraculously created an address book with mass e-mailing capability.

Fortunately for my own career, though, I've learned over the past few years that the various networking techniques out there are a matter of temperament. Some people love meeting new people, recording their contact information in databases, and then making matches between folks who want stuff and folks who have stuff to offer. Malcolm Gladwell, in *The Tipping Point*, calls these folks "connectors." Most networking books tell you how to become one.

Me? I know I'm too shy and disorganized to become such a person. So I've developed my own techniques. For instance, I migrate to existing electronic networks, like Princeton's alumni e-mail lists or the American Society of Journalists and Authors "Phorum." I also seek out nonprofessional networks, like the choirs I sing in. Somebody else has assembled these networks for me, and

I don't have to deal with the awkwardness of making small talk at cocktail parties in order to ask these people for help and to help them out when I can.

I also make sure to meet people who like being connectors. Then I hover like an outer planet in orbit around them. For some reason, they seem to tolerate me. They lend me their networks when I need them. I wind up needing them a lot.

If you want to build a career outside the grind, you, too, will soon discover that a functioning network is your best bet for avoiding calamity. Though I hate the word and the slick "let me give you my card" interactions that it conjures up, I've learned that networking is crucial for learning anything, or getting anything done.

That's because life is not like school. When we were in school, knowledge existed in books or in preassembled course packets and in one person, the teacher. Knowledge also existed in discrete areas called subjects. You could be fairly sure that you would not have to learn to write computer code in order to succeed in an English class. If by some random chance you did have to do this, you would be warned well in advance and given the proper materials to learn coding. Those are the rules of the school game.

Outside school, though, the rules change. Knowledge still exists in books, sure, but you have to figure out which books. You have to assemble your own "course packets" from the resources on the Internet, magazine and newspaper articles, peer-reviewed studies, government and industry data sources, or unsubstantiated blog rants and e-mail forwards if you want. Knowledge still exists in people, but you have to figure out which people. Some are trustworthy and competent, and some are not. Unlike the teacher, who is paid to answer your questions, competent, trustworthy people may or may not return your calls. It helps if you know someone who knows them.

> **If you want to build a career outside the grind, you, too, will soon discover that a functioning network is your best bet for avoiding calamity. Though I hate the word and the slick 'let me give you my card' interactions that it conjures up, I've learned that networking is crucial for learning anything, or getting anything done.**

Adding to the complications, when you strike out on your own, you have to learn constantly. This is even more true when you are young and don't know anything. You have to figure out what you don't know and train your mind to leap across vastly different areas. As a freelance writer, there have been weeks when I've had to become an expert on everything from the economics of massive multiplayer online games to luxury handbags to Kosher for Passover travel packages.

I'm not the only independent worker who's had to become a Jill of all trades—and had to learn to sort through the good and bad information out there.

Alex Freedman, cofounder of the essay editing service With Honors, tells me that when he and business partner Austin Brentley started their company, they soon learned that increasing their market share was all about boosting their search engine rankings. So they searched extensively online and found some consulting firms that promised to help them do this. Alas, not all were equally helpful. They hired one firm based in India. That firm kept delaying and not doing the work. Then they hired an American firm. This company created phony Web pages linking to With Honors. That drew the ire of Google, which blacklisted the site for a bit by setting the page rank to zero. Chastened, the With Honors team hired another Indian firm, which helped the company boost its rank through more legitimate means, like adding new content and asking people to link to the site. (Though Freedman and Brentley didn't tap their networks to find this last company, I've discovered that one of a network's best functions is helping you figure out whom you can trust to do a good job.)

Meanwhile, they'd hired a Russian programmer to build the back end of the With Honors site. This would allow the company's essay editors to log in, post their availability, and receive essays as clients sent them. The programmer built the program from scratch. That was a rather laborious process. Unfortunately, the programmer decided it was too laborious, and turned in an incomplete program with 10,000 lines of code. "We freaked out," says Freedman. "We had no money, no budget. We had a Web site that could receive traffic, but no back end." The only thing they could do was call on their network of friends for help. They got in touch with two of their computer whiz buddies from college. One looked at the dizzying 10,000 lines and basically said, "Sorry to hear about this—good luck!" The other said about the same thing ("Wow, this is 10,000 lines of code!").

"That was the lowest of low points," Freedman says. Fortunately, the second programmer called back a few hours later and said he'd looked over the program and thought he could help. He spent approximately 100 hours debugging the software over the next few weeks. With Honors was on its way.

So that he would never be caught in that situation again, Freedman decided to learn how to code. He read over the lines that the Russian programmer had written and learned how to follow the pathways. He hunted on the Internet for examples of coding fixes and formats. After two years, he's well versed enough in computer programming to fix any problems the site has on the front or back end. With Honors' sales have doubled in each of the past two years. Without the two key ingredients in Grindhopper training—a network and the ability to learn on the fly (i.e., a "nimble mind")—this would not have been possible.

BUILDING A NETWORK

At its most fundamental level, a network consists of people whose opinions and expertise you have reason to trust, and whom you're more likely to help than a person off the street.

Many networks are informal—your neighbor, for instance, or the mailman with the great teeth who gives you the name of his dentist. There's a lot to be said for these free-flowing networks. Their informal nature, however, and their nebulous boundaries and memberships make them challenging to navigate. Formal groups have more defined norms. Members opt in. They join expecting to meet people who can help them and to help other members. Building a career outside the grind requires meeting

> **At its most fundamental level, a network consists of people whose opinions and expertise you have reason to trust, and whom you're more likely to help than a person off the street.**

lots of people who are willing to help you. For that reason, you should seek out a few groups to join, even if you're on the shy side, like me.

You can, of course, join as many networking groups as you want. But finding or building each of four types of networks will help you gain maximum leverage with minimal e-mail frenzy:

> 1 *Coworkers:* A small "strong ties" industry group
>
> 2 *Buddies:* A small "strong ties" nonindustry group
>
> 3 *Colleagues:* A big "weak ties" industry group
>
> 4 *A web:* A big "weak ties" nonindustry group

"Strong ties" means that you meet regularly, you all know one another's names and family situations, and you basically consider one another friends. There are no degrees of separation between the members of strong ties groups. Any member can call and just start speaking to another with no introduction needed.

"Weak ties" means that you may not know all the members of the network personally, but you could introduce yourself as a member of the network and thus create a tie if the need arose. Most members of these networks are one or two degrees of separation from each other (they are friends of friends).

A "strong ties" industry group—the first network—would be a group like the Austin Craft Mafia (profiled in Grindhopping Guideline 1). These nine women all know one another, talk one another up to reporters, and try to create sales opportunities for one another. They're all in the same industry, though since it's a creative industry, they're not direct competitors. That's why I call them coworkers. They know what each member is going through with her business and her career. That can be important for Grindhoppers who work by themselves, whether they're writing in a garret some-where or sewing guitar straps in a basement workshop. Having a small group of such coworkers makes you feel like part of a team.

The second network, your buddies, is just as important. These are people you know and trust who are not necessarily in your industry. Some might be, but you all have another shared interest. For instance, I sing in a choir of young urban professionals called the Young New Yorkers' Chorus. Our primary purpose is to make beau-tiful music together. Our secondary purpose is to imbibe large quan-tities of beer at local pubs after rehearsal. It's very relaxed. There are no sweep-the-business-card-out-of-the-pocket moments. But if someone needs help finding an apartment, a date, or a job, all she has to do is ask. We will tap our networks to assist if we can.

These non-career-oriented groups are sometimes even more helpful professionally than industry groups. Not only do the other members know and trust you, but you're quite likely to be the only person in your industry that they know. Lisa Huff, a Boulder, Colorado–based artist, told me that she prioritized joining a local businesswomen's group over finding an artists' group for this specific reason. Artists don't buy paintings. Businesswomen do. Small church groups and kickball teams are also good this way. They're even better if they feature people who are different ages from you. Older people are more likely to know folks in positions of influence, and since you're a friend, they won't mind introducing you. As a younger person, sometimes you're less likely to be in a position to pay these favors back, but if you can, you will. If you can't, being profusely and genuinely thankful usually does the trick as well.

Big "weak ties" industry groups—your colleagues—are the garden-variety professional organizations that everyone tells you to join. The better ones feature Internet forums or chat rooms, newsletters, annual conferences, and maybe online classes. If you're short on cash for membership fees, join the most selective organization you're eligible for. Snobby? Sure. But you'll get more out of it. When I decided to make freelance writing my career, I joined the American Society of Journalists and Authors because it required people to have been published in national newspapers or magazines or else have written a few books. For a writer, people who write for the *New York Times Magazine* are more useful resources than people who write for *Southeast Air Conditioner Repair Weekly*. Also, I feel more comfortable recommending members for projects if I know that they have a certain level of credibility.

That level of credibility is what makes college alumni networking groups so popular in the last category, non-industry-oriented weak ties groups. You may not know the people in these networks personally, but you know they have something in common with you (an alma mater) and a certain level of competence (or at least they managed to fool the admissions committee). Some companies, such as McKinsey and Goldman Sachs, also maintain alumni networks for people who once worked there, but then left for other things. From their perches in different companies, industries, and even walks of life, these loosely connected people help one another find jobs, clients, and plumbers. And yes, they gossip about former coworkers or classmates. Who says networking has to be all work?

WORKING YOUR NETWORKS

You don't have to be a connector to use connections. Like me, Chinwe Onyeagoro is "the worst person at power networking," she says. You won't find her working cocktail parties, partly because they turn her off, and partly because the people she needs to meet in her business don't hang out at cocktail parties. They're also not particularly impressed by the fact that she graduated from Harvard, or that she worked for McKinsey after graduation (though both of those institutions have excellent weak-tie alumni networks).

Onyeagoro's family immigrated from Nigeria shortly before she was born. She spent only a year of her childhood in Nigeria, when she was four. But the stories her parents and siblings told left a larger impression of this country in her mind than her time there would imply. Her entire education and career have been built around her goal of returning to sub-Saharan Africa someday to help build her ancestral homeland.

At Harvard, Onyeagoro studied economics and East Asian studies to see if Nigeria could learn anything from how the "Five Tigers"—Japan, South Korea, Taiwan, Hong Kong, and Singapore—developed. She went to McKinsey to learn how to solve problems rapidly. While working as a consultant in the Chicago office, she started buying properties in underdeveloped neighborhoods and renovating them. That taught her about the nitty-gritty aspects of improving communities. After two years at McKinsey, she left to work at the Pritzker Realty Group, a family real estate development company in Chicago, to make connections in that business. While there, she decided that she wanted to be involved in the whole community redevelopment process by working with politicians and community development corporations. The question was how.

"Chicago is all about introductions," she says. Local political officials were wary of this very young, very pedigreed woman from a real estate company who waltzed in to talk about improving their neighborhoods. One Chicago alderman actually threw her out of her office.

But Onyeagoro is "very focused on where I need to be, why I need to be there, what I'm trying to get out of a situation, and what I want to give back." She knew that once she gained the respect of Chicago's public officials and institutional leaders, they would make valuable introductions for her. Politicians, by their nature, are connectors with a wide range of relationships. So she went back to the alderman who'd thrown her out with a McKinsey-style PowerPoint presentation on the community goals the alderman had identified. She showed her how she could help meet these goals. She was also up front with her story: that she was a Nigerian woman who wanted to learn how to develop local economies so that she could go to Nigeria and do the same thing. The alderman warmed up. She didn't throw her out. Onyeagoro kept coming back to meet with her until she got the right introductions and the funding to work on one particular community development project.

After that, she formed a consulting company to do similar projects around Chicago, merging with another woman who had more experience in transportation and funding issues to become OH Community Partners. When I talked to Onyeagoro recently, OH Community Partners was working with everyone from the Regional Transportation Authority, which is the institution that oversees and funds public transit throughout northeastern Illinois, to the developers of a $60 million residential condominium and retail tower. Through her projects, Onyeagoro has gained the respect of a number of political officials and community leaders. In order to acquire new clients now, she identifies the decision makers that she needs to meet. Then she reaches out to influential people within her network and requests introductions to those decision makers. They are usually happy to oblige. "This approach has helped tremendously," she says.

Some people do like to make databases of everyone they know and work the cocktail party circuit to collect more business cards. But Onyeagoro's story shows that you don't have to be that kind of person to work a network.

> **"Certain people know more people than others. If you impress them, they'll open doors for you."**

Certain people know more people than others. If you impress them, they'll open doors for you.

When you're young and you haven't had years to build the databases that networking books talk about, this is not a bad way to go.

So how do you meet these decision makers and connectors? First, you figure out who they are. You do this by asking people you know who are knowledgeable about that particular field, by reading newspaper articles to see who's quoted, or even by just Google searching to see who is referenced most. Then, if you don't have an acquaintance in common, you meet these people by politely e-mailing them, calling them, or just showing up, as Onyeagoro did. Done right (i.e., don't interrupt a CEO you want to meet while she's having a romantic dinner with her husband), this works with almost anyone—even famous, busy connector people. Sometimes we forget that these people actually like to meet people. They particularly like to meet smart, polite young people who want to learn.

Eric Kutner, a sports marketing entrepreneur, found that to be the case. Before college, he was very interested in the research, design, and development of athletic footwear. In particular, he was fascinated by Nike. At age 16, he convinced his mother to purchase Nike stock, which turned out to be a smart financial decision (the price quadrupled over the next decade). As a college sophomore, he attended the U.S. Open tennis finals and saw Nike's founder and CEO, Phil Knight, seated in the VIP section. He decided to work his way down from the upper deck of the Louis Armstrong Stadium to the section where Knight had viewed the match. Finally, he got close enough to meet him. "I introduced myself," Kutner says. "I explained that I was studying physics at Princeton, and explained my appreciation for his company. He told me to find him after I graduated. Three years later, again at the U.S. Open, I worked my way 'downstairs' to reintroduce myself to Mr. Knight. He was very gracious and remembered meeting me. He introduced me to several Nike marketing people and suggested that, if I were able to attend the upcoming annual meeting at Nike's headquarters in Beaverton, Oregon, he would connect me with his executive assistant, who would set me up with human resources informational meetings and interviews. I have visited Nike's headquarters many times since then and met with Mr. Knight on most of these trips. The contacts I have made thanks to him have been invaluable."

Youth, in the business world, is the equivalent of a letter of introduction.

A slightly more complicated method of meeting people, though one with a high success rate, is to organize an event and invite the people you want to meet as presenters.

Fern Reiss took this approach. A "serial entrepreneur with ADD," in her words, Reiss is currently running a business called Expertizing, which helps clients earn better media placement. At one point, she says, "I decided I wanted to meet more business magazine editors—both so that I could pitch them my latest businesses and those of my clients—so I put together a panel discussion of several top business editors from *Inc.* magazine, *Fortune*, and *Harvard Business Review*." She ran it through an entrepreneurial organization in Boston. "The program was so successful I'll probably do a repeat with different journalists and editors next year. So it's a win-win for everyone; the audience loved it, the journalists are happy to participate, and instead of scrambling to 'network' with these editors, I'm the program moderator and organizer—so I took them all out for dinner." No hovering outside a conversation group at a cocktail party or 5,000-name database was necessary.

On the other hand, if you are a connector, you can make an excellent low-capital business out of your network. People will pay dearly to avoid the hassles of finding vendors or experts themselves.

Rebecca Miller, a caricature artist, is one such connector. When she was growing up, she always had a crayon or pencil in her hand. She started drawing portraits at an amusement park in Allentown, Pennsylvania, to earn some cash the summer before she enrolled at the Rhode Island School of Design. She soon discovered that she had a knack for capturing people's quirks and charms. For the next several years, she drew caricatures at parties and festivals in her spare time to help finance her education and world travels. She even sketched faces she saw on the streets of Ghana, Nepal, and Guatemala to keep her drawing skills sharp.

After getting laid off from her textile design job in 2002, Miller decided to turn her caricature-drawing hobby into a full-time business. She named her company NYSketches. Business grew quickly, but she soon noticed a problem: everyone who wants a caricature artist wants one at the same time (weekend afternoons and evenings). So she started contracting out to other caricature artists. Sometimes clients would ask if she knew other kinds of entertainers they could hire, from balloon artists to clowns to magicians. Miller decided to expand the mission of NYSketches to become a talent bank of such entertainers.

If you call, Miller and her business partner Henoch Getz can arrange for any combination of entertainers to show up at your son's bar mitzvah. That's one side of their network. They have built this network by asking friends of friends for recommendations, meeting actors and dancers at parties, and realizing who has a talent for making other people feel festive.

They're also, increasingly, building a network on the client side of NYSketches. This network consists of event planners and other marketers who tap into Miller and Getz's connections to help them stage events. For instance, the marketing/advertising agency representing Lexus hired several NYSketches artists to ply their trades at the 2005 U.S. Open in Queens (which Lexus was sponsoring). Miller and Getz made sure to maintain that contact through the year. Sure enough, the same person at the agency contacted them recently to see if they knew anyone who could draw caricatures in Los Angeles at the Lexus Jazz Festival in May. They did—and took their cut for arranging the booking.

They also worked with the marketing coordinator of Sandals Resorts recently to create a festive atmosphere at the company's *New York Times* Travel Show booth in February 2006. Sandals Resorts wanted to promote its family-friendly destinations. Having balloon artists and magicians on hand seemed like a good way to do that. There's no reason Sandals couldn't have hired these performers directly, but marketing coordinators for big resorts have other things to do with their time than cold-call guys who know how to walk on stilts. It was easier and quicker to go through a talent bank.

That "easier and quicker" aspect is a big benefit that connectors can deliver to their clients. In essence, NYSketches is a network with Miller and Getz as its hub. About the only capital they needed to launch their business was cash for a Web site. Here, "web"—a joining spot for connected people—really is the right word to use.

HOW TO LEARN

Since knowledge is often found in people, building a network and a nimble mind go hand in hand. Your network is going to be one of the first places you go when you need to learn something for building your career outside the grind.

Has another essay-editing service snapped up a domain name that's a slight variation on your company's name? Post a question on your college networking e-mail list asking for the name of an intellectual property lawyer who has an affinity for start-ups.

Make sure you don't reinvent the wheel. Whatever the issue you're facing, someone else has faced a similar challenge before. Do an Internet search on the subject that's currently vexing you. That's how Alex Freedman of With Honors figured out how to fix some of the coding bugs in his company's software.

Read everything you can. If you're a jewelry designer, and you're planning to sell your creations online, there are several books on setting up online stores or selling through established channels such as eBay. They will talk you through the process. Reading also helps you keep up in your field and helps you find the answers to basic questions. Finding simple answers this way means that you don't need to bug your network constantly. So make time for reading, no matter how busy you are. I know one doctor who keeps up with his specialty by reading medical journal articles in the bathroom. It's not a bad technique.

> **Since knowledge is often found in people, building a network and a nimble mind go hand in hand. Your network is going to be one of the first places you go when you need to learn something for building your career outside the grind.**

Don't be shy about bugging people with harder questions, though. Ben Baumann is the cofounder of Isovera, a technology consulting company that works with nonprofits. A few years ago, he and his business partner decided to hatch a new company, Akaza Research, that would provide a technology platform called OpenClinica to help academic medical centers track clinical trial data. The Isovera team knew a lot about technology, but they didn't know a lot about pharmaceutical trials.

So they decided to learn. They read everything they could. They spent a year picking the brains of medical researchers about what they needed and what could be done. They asked experts to come speak to the company about papers they'd written. People were flattered by such requests and usually offered to help. They spent a lot of time talking to potential customers to nail down the details of how clinical trials worked. "You learn to ask the right questions," Baumann says. "You learn to talk to the right people."

The Isovera team also took classes to beef up their knowledge of drug research. In case it's not obvious from the rest of this book, I'm not a big fan of graduate degrees, except for the degrees that certain professions require you to have (e.g., a medical degree to be a doctor). Too often, companies insist that certain positions require a master's degree for no better reason than that it makes the position seem more elite. But that's not to say that individual courses in specific areas where you lack knowledge can't be helpful. You can audit university courses if you want to relive the college experience without incurring the debt that people trying to re-create college through graduate school take on. Personally, I like taking courses online, rather than in person. That way, you don't need to waste time traveling anywhere. Of course, taking online courses requires self-discipline. No one makes you do anything, and there's not even the discomfort factor of facing the teacher when you know you've done a lousy job. If you're a Grindhopper, though, you're already self-disciplined. That makes online courses an excellent option.

You can also take "courses" by working in the grind for a bit. Maybe you're putting in a year or two to build up some savings or pay off student loans. Instead of thinking of your job as a place where you're biding your time, think of it as earning a degree in business practices. Chinwe Onyeagoro worked at McKinsey and the real estate company to learn things she thought she would need in her later career as a Grindhopper. If you're working in a big corporation, make a point of meeting people in different functions. Grill the HR folks on how they hire people. Pick the sales guys' brains on how to land new clients. Study the in-house counsel's negotiating techniques. Some Grindhoppers told me that approaching their first job with this level of detachment enabled them to deal better with certain annoying aspects of the grind. You're not a lifer. You're taking what you can while you can. Rather than hoarding office supplies, though, you're hoarding knowledge while you collect a paycheck.

Even if you soak up as much of an industry as is humanly possible in two years in the grind, though, you can never learn everything. That's why Grindhoppers don't just try to collect knowledge. They learn how to learn. Cultivating a nimble mind means building mental pathways that enable you to gather random bits of information like puzzle pieces and fit them together. You learn to solve problems. You learn to solve them quickly.

You cultivate a nimble mind the same way you cultivate a nimble body, namely, by putting it through a training regimen that keeps it limber. You can push this process along by reading things that are unrelated to your field to stretch your mind. Read a newspaper every day. Read a magazine every week, preferably in something you know nothing about, like *Popular Mechanics* or, if you are a mechanic, *Real Simple*. Read a book every month (these last three ideas have the added benefit of keeping people like me in business). Do crossword puzzles or play trivia games to cultivate your ability to pull up information from your mental files. Shake up your daily routine to force your brain into active mode. Exercise to "jog" thoughts loose. Carry around a notebook to write your thoughts down. Meet two or three smart friends for lunch and brainstorm ideas over sandwiches. Marry someone smart and turn dinner and pillow talk into idea-generating moments. You don't have to be on all the time. But like our bodies, our brains stay in better condition when we work them out regularly.

Smart people love to learn. Don't lose the habit just because you're not in school anymore.

Above all, have confidence that you will learn what you need to know. Most Grindhoppers have told me that if they'd actually sat down at the beginning of their grind-free careers and thought about all the things they'd have to learn, they would have freaked out. But along the way, they learned to write code, figure out what an "LLC" is and how you become one, find out who sells film production insurance, find out how clinical trials work, run a payroll system for 20 people, or whatever else they needed to. You'll leverage your network and your nimble mind until you come up with something satisfactory. You get better as you go.

> **Smart people love to learn. Don't lose the habit just because you're not in school anymore.**

I discovered this recently when I had to deal with a massive project. I needed to write a draft of a book on building a rewarding career without paying your dues, based on interviews with Grindhoppers who'd done it. I wanted a reasonable mix of men and women, locations and ethnicities, and I wanted mostly nonsoftware entrepreneurs. We'd heard those stories during the dot-com boom. I wanted more colorful tales. How would I find these people and enough information to put between the best stories to make a 60,000-word book?

I used every method described in this chapter. First I tapped my "strong ties" networks. About two years ago, a woman who sat next to me in choir (who happened to be a magazine editor) gave me a mint from a strange, sleek tin that said "Oral Fixation." She mentioned that the founders were young and I might find them interesting. I did. I wrote about them and a few other entrepreneurs for

147

ay. When I decided to do a book on the topic, I went back
repreneurs in my story and asked them if I could use their
stories again.

Then I asked if they knew anyone I should contact. They did. For
instance, the Oral Fixation guys had just worked with Ron Shah's
Jina Ventures. Shah turned out to be a classic connector. Not only
did he have a good story, he had a list of eight other people I should
call. Every time I bumped into one of these connectors while
working on this book, I felt like I'd hit the jackpot. Some contacted
me to see if I'd be interested in interviewing them. Then halfway
through the interview, they'd stop and say, "Hey, do you need more
names?" Others just wanted to be helpful. For instance, I had dinner
with Helen Coster, a reporter at *Forbes*, to tell her about my project.
She told me that I should e-mail Marci Alboher, a connector-type
author who was also working on a career book. Alboher opened her
Rolodex and found me Ryan Nerz, the competitive eating circuit
judge, and Rebecca Miller, the NYSketches owner and caricature
artist profiled in this chapter.

Meanwhile, I posted a notice on the Princeton Venture Net e-mail
list saying that I was looking for interview subjects. Dozens of folks
e-mailed me—some about themselves, and some about non-Princeton
friends that I just *had* to call. That's how I found people like Tom
Szaky of TerraCycle, Greg Galant, the podcast consultant, and
Brittany Blockman and Josephine Decker, the documentary film-
makers I profiled in Grindhopping Guideline 2.

A similar question put to fellow members of the American
Society of Journalists and Authors landed me the names of the
Austin Craft Mafia, videographer Justin "Red" Sanders, and Sarah
Doyle Lacamoire, the Scotch expert, among others.

Then, a few weeks later, I posted a completely unrelated note on
a writing e-mail list that mentioned my Web site in the tag. A
Harvard Law School grad named Anthony Hong read the post,
followed the link to my Web site, and read about my Grindhopping
project. He asked if I would like him to post a blurb about my book
on Harvard's law and business networking lists. Bingo, another
connector! Hong also posted my request for interview subjects on
The Square, another "weak ties" multicollege networking Web site.
Dozens more leads came in. That's how I found Chinwe Onyeagoro,
Syl Tang of HipGuide, and Hayden Hamilton, the drug importer,
among other people.

I sought out some people myself. I read about Mena and Ben Trott of Six Apart in a magazine profile. I asked for an introduction to LeUyen Pham after her neighbor mentioned on another e-mail list that she was a phenomenal illustrator. I read about sand sculpting as a business in Barbara Winter's *Making a Living without a Job*. I found statistics by asking what questions I'd like answered, then hunting on Bureau of Labor Statistics, Small Business Administration, and Census Bureau sites or calling these offices until I found answers. I found what I could in other books, from Daniel Pink's *Free Agent Nation* to Meshel's *One Phone Call Away*. To track down Elizabeth Murray, the colonial Grindhopper in the chapter on Grindhopping Guideline 1, I e-mailed the author of a scholarly book on small business history. He e-mailed me the names of two other academics who'd studied early American women business owners. Neither turned out to study the colonial period. But one did tell me that a historian named Patricia Cleary had written a book on a colonial business-woman. I tracked down Cleary's book and found Murray.

Suffice it to say, this is a different version of learning from the standard American History version of learning, where if you needed to know about a colonial American businesswoman, she'd be profiled in your textbook.

Grindhopping, on the other hand, requires you to learn like you're a reporter on assignment. You figure out what you need to know, how quickly you need to know it, who has that information, and how you get it from them.

You may also be spectacularly wrong (wrong enough to get Google to blacklist your essay-editing Web site), and there are no answers in the back of the book to tell you that. As one Grindhopper told me, learning outside school and outside the grind is like being in an attic in a dark house and trying to feel your way down to the front door. You stub your toe. You walk into the walls a few times. Then you start to develop a sense of where the doors should be and how tall the steps are. By the first floor, you pretty much know the floor plan.

> **Grindhopping requires you to learn like you're a reporter on assignment. You figure out what you need to know, how quickly you need to know it, who has that information, and how you get it from them.**

You still might stub your toe in the foyer. But if you're the kind of kid who got bored listening to lectures, you'll like this new way of learning. Your mind becomes as nimble as a cat burglar, creeping toward the light under the door that's just visible in the distance.

GRINDHOPPING

DEALING WITH THE DOWNSIDES

Yes, there are downsides to striking out on your own. There are the obvious ones, such as not having company-subsidized benefits and dealing with the headaches caused by Grindhopper-unfriendly taxes and paperwork. Then there are the less obvious downsides of creating your own brand in a brand-conscious society, becoming a good boss when you've never had a boss, and overcoming the natural "responsible" human tendency to put self-actualization toward the bottom of your to-do list. All are surmountable. Still, it's better to know that these downsides exist. That way, you can face them head on.

"BUT WHAT ABOUT HEALTH INSURANCE?"

That was the question many folks asked, alarmed, when I told them that I was writing a book about young freelancers and microbusiness owners. Some of them assumed that I must be writing about the horrible lack of benefits that independent contractor status implies. After all, that's what the Generational Spokespeople moan about when they note the rise in self-employment among the under-35 set.

But, like many things the Spokespeople claim, this assumption that all independent workers have health insurance woes is wrong.

Since I started working for myself, I've never lacked health insurance. That's not a risk I'm willing to take. I value having money in the bank, and there's nothing like an appendectomy, a brutal mugging, or a ski accident—all things I've seen 20-something friends experience in the last few years—to make savings disappear.

Now, I won't pretend that I didn't enjoy the extra space that getting married and going on my husband's health insurance plan created in my budget. And I won't pretend that the cost of health insurance doesn't stifle some entrepreneurial spirits.

But it doesn't have to. When I lived in Washington, D.C., right out of college, I found a temporary catastrophic health insurance plan. Mine cost me $800 a year; searching on eHealthInsurance.com and other online sites, I've found rates in other states for as low as $69 a month for (permanent) $5,000 deductible policies. Check out TONIK policies in California, Colorado, and a few other states for examples of such low-cost plans. When you're young and healthy, catastrophic insurance is a reasonable bet. You're covered if you have a major illness or accident, and if you want to go to the doctor or need prescriptions, you just pay cash. Some doctors actually prefer taking cash to dealing with health insurance companies. Unless you spend more than $500 a year on doctors (about the cost of two visits) or more than $100 a month on prescriptions, the cost to bump up to a policy that covers visits and prescriptions will be greater than the cost of the services you need. If you do purchase a catastrophic insurance plan, be sure to stash some money away every month in an account that you can access to pay the deductible, should the need arise.

Sometimes it's not possible to purchase a cheap catastrophic insurance plan. After I moved to New York City, I learned that New York's regulations at the time made it difficult for insurance companies to offer these sorts of deals to individuals. As a result, I had to sign up for an HMO.

Fortunately, I found an organization offering group rates that I could join. Signing up as part of a group is usually the way to go when you buy HMOs, PPOs, and other insurance policies of this ilk. When you buy noncatastrophic insurance as an individual, insurance companies assume that there's a moral hazard issue involved, especially if you are not currently insured. Perhaps you have just been diagnosed with a major illness or have just discovered that you are pregnant, and you are signing up for insurance to sock someone else with the bills. In some states, insurers can decline to issue a policy to an individual for just about any reason, and coming as an individual might qualify as a reason. Or you might get stuck with really high rates or big exclusions on preexisting or subsequent conditions. When you buy as a group, insurance companies assume that the risk is spread, and premiums tend to be lower.

So do your due diligence and work your network to find some group you can join that offers group health insurance rates. This can be a professional organization, a state-sponsored organization, a small business consortium, or some similar group. I landed my policy through the Freelancers Union, which operates in New York. My first year, I paid $255 a month. The second year, I paid $286 a month. I checked the Web site for current New York rates (in spring 2006) and found that they run from $113.91 a month for the equivalent of a catastrophic plan for individuals to $879.12 per month for a rather generous family HMO plan (two parents and multiple children) with $20 office co-pays, drug coverage, and free well-child care. If they were willing to take a catastrophic plan, families could land coverage for $373.89 a month; a midsized deductible insurance plan for a married couple would run $263.81 a month.

Those are the numbers for self-employed folks or microbusiness owners in New York, one of the most expensive areas of the country. If you're self-employed, you can usually deduct your premiums as a business expense, meaning that the price feels lower.

When you look at the numbers in black and white, the health insurance situation isn't *that* scary. Would I have rather spent $286 a month on clothes or a better apartment? Sure. Some self-employed types do spend the cash that they could devote to premiums on clothes or eating out—and then claim that health insurance is too expensive. It isn't. It's a matter of making choices.

Most people wouldn't take a job they hated rather than a job they loved just because it paid $3,432 more a year. Paying for your own health insurance requires making that same choice.

This calculation works with any perk, really, from free coffee to in-cubicle massages. Google, according to a recent *Time* magazine profile, gives workers three free gourmet meals a day at the company's Mountain View, California, headquarters. Bear in mind that offering free dinner is a good way to get people to work late, and salaried Google workers aren't earning overtime. Those meals may pay for themselves. But say you envy that as a perk. Simply research what it costs to purchase a gourmet meal delivery service for three meals, five days a week. At Zone Chefs and NuKitchen, meals run about $40 a day, or $200 for a work week. Multiply to find the yearly cost ($10,000), then build this into your rates. Don't whine that people in the corporate world don't have to make this trade-off. Money that's going for free meals isn't going into employees' salaries or boosting returns and hence the stock price in their 401(k). And really, even a $10,000 perk might come with a lifestyle cost that exceeds the actual dollar amount. Most Grindhoppers aren't willing to work somewhere they don't want to, under conditions they don't like, for $40 worth of extra goodies daily. They'd rather cook their own meals.

> **"Most people wouldn't take a job they hated rather than a job they loved just because it paid $3,432 more a year. Paying for your own health insurance requires making that same choice."**

But back to benefits. If you work for yourself, buy a catastrophic plan if you're eligible (and healthy). Check Web sites such as eHealthInsurance.com for rates. If you're not so healthy, or if you can't find a catastrophic plan in your state, check which professional organizations you can join that offer group rates on health insurance. If you want to offer health insurance for your employees, some state governments are starting to offer group pools for businesses that are too small to qualify for their own reasonable group rates. If you're just purchasing a policy for yourself, and you wind up with a high deductible, that's okay. That's what insurance should be, anyway: insuring against low-probability, high-cost events, not against high-probability, low-cost events like going to the doctor. If you've got a preexisting condition like diabetes, you may need to play the health insurance game a little differently in some states. Check with your doctor or patient advocacy groups for information and advice. But most young, healthy Grindhoppers need not suppress any entrepreneurial longings because of the cost of benefits.

THE PITA FACTOR

Though people don't think about this downside as much, I think the PITA factor is a bigger problem for Grindhoppers than the lack of subsidized health insurance. I use PITA in the headline because I'm a prude. PITA stands for "pain in the ass." When you work for a big company, someone else handles the tax paperwork, the various business licenses you need, regulatory procedures, even dealing with utilities, the post office, and watering the plants. Unless your Grindhopping business gets pretty big, when you work for yourself, you'll be dealing with all these things.

And dealing with them *is* a pain in the posterior. Our society is set up for big companies and people who work for big companies. Think taxes. Like all freelancers, I pay both the employer and employee parts of my social security taxes. Since I think the system is a Ponzi scheme anyway, this makes me doubly mad. New York also requires me to pay something called an "unincorporated business tax," which I thought was a joke the first time I heard it. Here's the punch line: New York considers the fact that I work for myself in my own home to be a taxable activity beyond the income taxes I already pay to the city and state. I'd laugh if it didn't cost me over $1,500 last year. Some cities also have old laws that make home-based businesses difficult to establish legally, though they're as easy to start as turning on your computer.

If you want to start a limited liability company or some variety of corporation, or if you want to work in an office that's separate from your home, you're in for even more fun.

Christian Lerch and George Tsiatis, for instance, are starting an event production and marketing company called Group 113 in an office that used to be a Mexican restaurant. If you worked for a big company, building renovations would happen without your attention. Lerch and Tsiatis are ripping out the kitchen themselves, "fighting the cockroaches for control of the taqueria/office," as Lerch puts it. "Every day in the renovation process we come across the strange and unusual, including some very creative plumbing, some very old seafood . . ."

Then there's the paperwork. Lerch and Tsiatis learned that to become an LLC, not only did they have to pay a lawyer to file the papers and pay a filing fee, but they were also supposed to spend a significant amount of money announcing their intentions in a number of print publications. Now, as a person who writes for print,

I'm happy that business incorporation law has protected at least one source of ad revenue for my clients. But it does seem silly that a new business in this wired age would need to announce itself in a part of the newspaper that no one reads.

All these headaches can drive you crazy. The fees and rules in particular can drive you crazy, because the municipalities and governments that implement them benefit when people start new businesses within their borders. So why do so few make it easy or cheap for people to open these businesses?

Someday, the rise in microbusinesses and the competition between cities for talent may lead to the invention of a universal "new business packet"—a folder with all the laws you need to know and maybe two or three pieces of paperwork to file. But bureaucrats tend to be Organization types. So I'm not holding my breath.

The best I can say is that most Grindhoppers find that the ends justify the means. When I touched base with Lerch and Tsiatis a few weeks after our initial conversation, they had not only won the battle with the cockroaches (or at least hadn't seen one in 24 hours), they were working with several clients, from a Greek Orthodox Church to a pair of Brooklyn "creative visionaries" who were keen on staging underground events during the spring and summer. They were "honestly booked and couldn't be happier," Lerch told me (even if the Verizon DSL installation guys did insist that the basement bathroom was the only place they could run the wire).

WHAT DO YOU DO?

The other downsides are a bit fuzzier than the perks and the PITA stuff. In a previous chapter, I joked about male Grindhoppers who call themselves "CEO" when the company consists of the Grindhopper himself and a part-time receptionist who answers to "Mom." But I understand the impulse.

We live in a brand-conscious society. When you work for a big company with a sterling reputation, some of that reputation rubs off on you, even if you were the lousiest guy hired in the last five years. When you work for yourself or start a small business, it's tempting to try to create prestige, if for no other reason than to assure the person who's asking that you're legit.

Freelancers are especially sensitive to this. Okay, maybe not all freelancers. *I* am especially sensitive to this. Some people freelance after being laid off and before they find another job. There is absolutely nothing wrong with doing this. But as a result, "freelance" has become a code word for "unemployed" among a certain set of credentialed individuals. Then there's the subject matter of my work. Plenty of folks who've never published anything call themselves writers. That makes "freelance writer" a double whammy in the dubious job title category. So I'll be at a cocktail party and someone will ask what I do. I used to say, "I'm a writer," but then people's heads started spinning around, looking to see who was supporting me while I spent my days doing what they considered a hobby.

> **"We live in a brand-conscious society. When you work for a big company with a sterling reputation, some of that reputation rubs off on you, even if you were the lousiest guy hired in the last five years. When you work for yourself or start a small business, it's tempting to try to create prestige, if for no other reason than to assure the person who's asking that you're legit."**

So then I tried "journalist." Inevitably, someone asks, "Oh, for which publication?" Well, not one specific one. "Oh, so you're *freelance*." Those standing in the conversation circle raise their eyebrows. And then I'm back into a prestige conversation, mentioning the names of the publications I write for and possibly even my tax return to assure the listener that I make a good living, thank you. Contrast this sputtering with someone who works in the grind. That person can just say, "I work at Goldman Sachs" without that admission sparking a conversation about his legitimacy.

There's no good way around this. Grindhoppers who run small businesses can simply talk about those businesses. One day I'll concoct a good elevator speech. Until then, I'm learning to realize that any connotation that people assign to my work is their problem, not mine.

I'm also realizing that it's easier for me, as a woman, not to care too much about my job title. Women are not judged primarily on what they do for a living. Men are—both by other men and by women. That's as unfair as judging women on their looks, but it's also, unfortunately, true. A man who says he's the CEO of a graphics design firm will be treated differently at a party from someone who says he does freelance graphic design work from home. I hope that someday this will change. Until then, Grindhoppers can shake up cocktail parties by acting confused when people announce that they work at name-brand companies. "Oh," you might say, "but what do you *do?*" A lot of times the answer is, "Make PowerPoint slides about other people's insights." And then you can count your blessings that you call yourself boss.

THE PROBLEM OF EMPATHY

Calling yourself boss from the get-go—and building a career without paying your dues—is a lot of fun for the Grindhopper. But it has some social consequences. Other people have spent years paying their dues. Working with—or reporting to—someone who hasn't can breed resentment. In this book, I profiled some Grindhoppers who'd done their own thing, then come back into the corporate world at high levels. Grindhoppers who take this path may suddenly find themselves managing teams of older or more experienced people. Other Grindhoppers build businesses that grow to employ lots of people before the Grindhopper has reached an age when corporate types have many direct reports. These situations beg the question: if you've always been your own boss, how do you learn to become the respected boss of someone else?

> **Everyone wins when you view the employer-employee relationship as more of a partnership.**

The answer is the same way Grindhoppers learn everything: by trial and error and by asking everyone they know for advice—with a healthy dose of humility thrown in.

Laura Weidman cofounded Overqualified, a tutoring service, shortly after graduating from college. One of her first tasks was to hire 20 part-time tutors. People of all ages applied. So she hired people of all ages. Suddenly, she was managing folks much older than herself. The dynamics, she discovered, are challenging. "It's not just about 'I'm older, I have more experience, and I'm an authority figure, so listen to me,'" she says. "You can't just pull rank or take your authority for granted the way you could in a traditional job scenario. You have to really establish yourself as someone who knows what she's doing and cares about it, and you have to convey what you need in a very respectful way."

You get nowhere by coming in as the hotshot kid, even if you are the boss. You'll probably lose your best people if you do that, and hiring replacements is a real PITA.

Everyone wins when you view the employer-employee relationship as more of a partnership.

You bring certain things to the table, and your employees bring other things. Older employees, for instance, are great storehouses of knowledge. It's safe to assume that they know more than you do. They've seen someone else make that same stupid mistake you're about to make, and they'll steer you to safety—if you listen. As a manager, you then leverage that knowledge to help your whole team succeed.

> **"Yes, you will sometimes need to make unpopular decisions. But your employees should trust that you will explain the situation, keep them informed, be truthful, and otherwise treat them as you would want to be treated were the situation reversed."**

Yes, you will sometimes need to make unpopular decisions. But your employees should trust that you will explain the situation, keep them informed, be truthful, and otherwise treat them as you would want to be treated were the situation reversed.

This empathy—the capacity for participating in the feelings of another—is partly a matter of temperament. Some people naturally think of how other people perceive a situation. This is a great skill to have during negotiations or crisis management. Others of us learn. One of the ways we do so is by being observant. How do others react to certain words or body language? How might other people view you, and how does that compare with how you view yourself? You can't go crazy basing decisions on these perceptions, but they are data points to consider.

The other way we learn workplace empathy is by working in situations that we don't control. This is the one reason I worry about some Grindhoppers' forays into management. Many have never—even as kids—had jobs that sucked.

When I was a teenager, I wasn't savvy enough to know about cool summer research programs or how high school students might land scholarships for travel. So I found regular, old-fashioned, minimum-wage jobs to occupy my time. I spent one particularly garlicky summer working at an Italian fast-food restaurant. Standing on my feet for eight hours a day wasn't so bad. What I hated were the commands passed down from on high that required constant suggestive selling ("Would you like a salad with that?" even if all the person asked for was a Coke), or dictated that drive-through customers had to be acknowledged immediately (try that when you have to suggestive sell a salad to the three cars ahead of them in line). Corporate headquarters also issued guidelines requiring you to say your name to drive-through customers so that the customers would think you were friendly. Most people thought that 17-year-old Laura was just being nice. Some rather sketchy male customers, on the other hand, assumed that I must be interested in them, and was saying my name so that they'd know how best to hit on me when they pulled up to the window to pay and get their food. After this happened a few times, I got a little gun-shy about introducing myself and thus crossing the line into familiarity. But then I got yelled at by my coworkers, because the pay structure for everyone in the restaurant rode not on sales, but on the notes of three mystery guests who visited each month. These evaluators would dock the restaurant's score if the drive-through girl didn't act like she was your long-lost friend.

At first I wondered why the corporate honchos didn't realize that this would be an issue. But then I realized why. Every one of the restaurant's commands was dreamed up by someone who was not spending eight hours a day living with them. These restaurant executives had no empathy for actual restaurant workers.

I'm not going to write an ode to bad summer jobs here. I hated the experience. I probably would have learned a lot more about life if I'd figured out a way to travel to Africa each summer as part of a service mission or something. Also, my woes aren't particularly compelling. Billions of people have experienced much worse things than a crappy summer job. But my crappy jobs did give me a sense of the world that makes me think that the waitress has a lot of other stuff going on if she forgets my drink, not that she hates me.

As the competition to get into top colleges grows fiercer, though, fewer kids are spending their summers scribbling admissions essays in the parking lot during their smoke breaks. Some of these kids with no bad job memories will wind up as Grindhoppers. If they're not going to learn about what makes a good boss through bad jobs, they can try learning it through campus activities in college.

Campus activities were certainly helpful for Weidman. During college, she participated in a big undergraduate-run program that brought performing arts activities into local public schools. The first few years, she worked under the program directors and learned what made her feel motivated and what made her want to quit. Then she became a director of the program herself. She started managing teams of volunteers. As these volunteers had no reason beyond devotion to the cause to follow her lead and take direction, she had to learn to manage people both effectively and respectfully. It's a lesson that she took to Overqualified—and that she credits for helping her business grow.

EMBRACING THE UNSETTLED

The last downside is probably the trickiest. In Grindhopping Guideline 3, I noted that Grindhopping requires you to become comfortable with being uncomfortable. That chapter had guidelines on how to do that. In this chapter, I want to talk about why it's so difficult, on a psychological level, to make the leap from paychecks, corporate ladders, or even the regimented grades of school to a life of our own choosing. Grindhopping in its purest form requires reordering what psychologists call the *hierarchy of needs.*

This "hierarchy of needs" phrase comes from Abraham Maslow, a twentieth-century American psychologist who tried to counter some of the profession's worship of Freud. Rather than thinking that humans were captive to our Oedipal, castration, and whatever else complexes, Maslow postulated that the human psyche develops as we meet a series of needs. People first have to have their basic physical needs for food and shelter met. If we picture the hierarchy of needs as a pyramid, basic physical needs are the bottom layer. Then we need safety and security. That's the second layer. Then we need to feel love. Then we need to be held in esteem by other people. Then finally, at the top of the pyramid, comes self-actualization. We grow as we climb this hierarchy. First we avoid privation. Then, once we're safe and comfortable, loved and respected, we get to scream, "I'm me!"

Most people fit this ordering pretty well. Now that people in developed countries have achieved phenomenal standards of living, the bottom layer of the pyramid becomes a given for most individuals. That leaves the second layer, security, as the one of primary importance. Indeed, studies of the workforce find that job security is one of the most important factors, if not *the* most important factor, in job satisfaction. Headlines provide real-life evidence of this. As I'm writing this chapter, French young people are rioting over a proposal that would allow employers to fire workers under age 26 during their first two years on the job. The French youth unemployment rate is currently 23 percent. When companies can't fire people, as they can't easily in France, they don't hire people. It's too big a financial risk. But the French young people don't care. They want job security, even if they need to live on unemployment checks as a result.

French young people are worried about moving to an American-style system where, in the popular French imagination, people lose their jobs constantly. That's not an entirely accurate perception. Even with all the up-and-down economic news of the past few years, Americans feel reasonably secure in their jobs. A late 2005 Right Management Consultants survey found that only about 24 percent of U.S. workers said that it was very or somewhat possible that they would lose their jobs in the next 12 months. About half said that it was not at all possible. Maybe those folks are a tad optimistic, but given that most people feel secure, it's not surprising that the next level of the hierarchy, being part of a team, winds up being a highly desired job component in the American workforce. For many people, being part of a team is more important than long-term career advancement. One recent OfficeTeam survey found that 71 percent of employees would rather not switch jobs with their supervisors. Being the boss can be lonely. As William H. Whyte wrote in *The Organization Man*, people don't like to rise so high in the organization that their necks are outstretched for others to chop at.

A minority, of course, do want to climb up the corporate ladder to positions of prestige and responsibility. These ambitious people want to be held in esteem by others. Once they are, they start looking around for work with meaning. But few people are successful in this sphere. A 2005 Maritz poll found that only 20 percent of workers feel that their work gives them a strong sense of personal accomplishment. Only 10 percent strongly agreed that they look forward to going to work every day.

For most people, self-actualization is the icing on the career cake. It is something you work a lifetime for.

Even traditional schools of thought on entrepreneurship tell you that the middle layers of the hierarchy of needs should come first as you plan your life. In the first chapter of this book, I mentioned a young woman whose executive father told her that before she started a business, she needed to go to business school and work in industry for several years. In other words, she needed to build up significant assets (security), contacts (being part of a team), and a reputation (being held in esteem) before she could go out on her own.

> **Only 20 percent of workers feel that their work gives them a strong sense of personal accomplishment. Only 10 percent strongly agreed that they look forward to going to work every day. For most people, self-actualization is the icing on the career cake. It is something you work a lifetime for.**

Grindhoppers view the world differently. As with all human beings, their physical needs come first. It's hard to build a career without paying your dues if you're starving. But if you trust that you won't starve—and there's no reason to think you would if you're an intelligent person who can find resources if you need them—then Grindhoppers believe that the ordering of the other needs is up to you.

Grindhoppers put self-actualization first.

While they hedge their bets (building up savings, for instance), they do not need to be secure to make the leap. They get comfortable with being uncomfortable. They don't mind being part of a team (the third layer), but if being part of a team would compromise their vision, they put that need aside. Grindhoppers certainly like to be held in esteem. That's why I fumble over what to call myself at cocktail parties. That's why the young male CEOs of their one-person firms call themselves that. But Grindhoppers will also forgo the esteem of working at a brand-name company if it keeps them from living the life they want, even if the brand-name company promises to pay quite well.

Not everyone can or wants to do this. The Grindhopping revolution is a labor force split, not a shift. If security is what fundamentally makes you happy, then you won't be able to reorder your hierarchy of needs to put self-actualization at the top. Some people are perfectly happy with that, and some people have achieved perfect self-actualization at their "real" jobs.

If you're reading this book, though, that's probably not the case for you. A lot of the other guidelines in this book are for people who've already made the jump out of the grind. If you haven't, you may be wondering how you flip that magic switch that lets you reorder your needs. In my search for Grindhoppers, I interviewed a number of folks with good corporate jobs who were building dream businesses on the side. These young people asked me how they would know when it was okay to quit their jobs and pursue their passions. When would they be secure enough to reach toward the self-actualization they weren't finding in the grind?

That's the wrong question to ask. You'll never be secure enough. Even if you win the lottery, you can talk yourself into fretting about losing camaraderie or the prestige of your company's brand. You might get pushed. More than one person in the grind told me that he was hoping to be laid off because that would force him to figure out what he really wanted to do with his life. But if you are not easily cubicled, or if you don't think you'll find career bliss in someone else's cubicle, why phrase one of the most important questions of your life in a way that requires someone else to determine when you'll pursue what makes you happy?

Maybe it's time to ask a different question, about what kind of life you want. If you're in your 20s, chances are you have 60 years left on the planet. Since you've just read a book on not paying your dues—or skipped to the back—my guess is that you don't like to waste time. Using your remaining 60 years most effectively requires being true to your priorities. So be honest with yourself about what they are. Both self-actualization and the security-teamwork-esteem trifecta have upsides and downsides when you put one or the other on top.

I was reminded of this recently when I interviewed one of my most free-spirited Grindhoppers shortly after reading an eye-popping article in the March 1, 2006, *Wall Street Journal* called "Detroit's Symbol of Dysfunction: Paying Employees Not to Work."

It's no secret that the big American car companies have been falling apart lately. It's also no secret that their unionized workforces have structured their contracts to make security their top priority.

For the *Wall Street Journal* piece, reporter Jeffrey McCracken interviewed General Motors employees in Flint, Michigan, about something called the Jobs Bank. This two-decade-old program ensures that 15,000 auto workers continue to get paid during slow times when the companies do not need their services (for instance, if a plant is idled). The employees earn wages and benefits packages that often top $100,000 a year. To earn their salaries, workers must perform some company-approved activity. Most do volunteer projects or go to school. Some idled GM workers in Flint clock time in a place that workers call the "rubber room," which was the focus of the story.

McCracken interviewed a GM worker named Jerry Mellon who did a short stint in the rubber room in January. The room, Mellon reported, was a windowless old storage shed for engine parts. The employees assigned there had to show up at 6 a.m. every day and stay until 2:30 p.m., with 45 minutes off for lunch. A supervisor signed people out when they wanted to use the restroom.

Mellon joined GM in 1972. For years, he held jobs designing electronic systems for vehicle prototypes. Then in 2000, GM merged two divisions, and he lost his position. Since then, except for a short stint in 2001, GM has been paying him over $60,000 a year, plus benefits, not to work.

During that time, he's taken classes on how to do crossword puzzles and how to play Trivial Pursuit. He took classes for a bit at the Royal Flush Academy, an institute in Flint that trains people to work in casinos. Mellon wasn't interested in casino work, though, so when he quit that program, he had to report to the rubber room. For a week, he woke up at 4:30 a.m. to commute there. He read newspapers and took naps. He marveled at the guys who'd been in the rubber room for a lot longer than he had. Mellon said that a "line-worker mentality" kept people in the habit of showing up despite the pointlessness. "A lot of guys sit in that room and just collect their paycheck because they don't know what else to do," he told McCracken. "They've spent 20 years tightening a nut as it came down the line. They are faced with this harsh reality, and they are just happy the paycheck still comes so they can put their kid through college."

Idled GM workers have security. They've got a team in their union. They're still getting paid—and paid well—by a prestigious, brand-name company. They can achieve self-actualization as a side benefit through volunteer work, or even just by reading what they want in the rubber room. You could write a novel in there.

And yet, I shuddered when I read this story. I could not imagine doing make-work projects for years on end. I could not imagine spending my life waiting for a call to come back to work, even if I was paid well for my time, and even if I did have financial obligations. Money can be earned in other ways. I agree with Maslow that "if work is meaningless, then life comes close to being meaningless."

Obviously, most people's work features more meaning than the rubber room. But, remember, only 10 percent of Americans say that they really look forward to going to work every day. If you shudder at *that* statistic—at the idea that work will mean going somewhere and doing something you are supposed to, five days a week for the next 40 years—maybe you'll prefer the priorities of a tiny company called Maui Surfer Girls.

Dustin Ashley Tester, the founder of this camp for young women, told me shortly after I read the "rubber room" article that she has no 401(k), or a savings account, for that matter. Her salary doesn't approach that of the idled GM workers. Her business is at breakeven. She's been around for half a decade now, but the business has been "a roller coaster of good years and bad."

On the other hand, Tester has loved surfing since she was a little girl. Her dad introduced her to the sport. He pushed her into her first waves at Puamana Beach Park when she was eight, and he encouraged her to dive off a 15-foot cliff at Kaanapali's "Black Rock" when she was only nine. During one of those early sessions, he pointed to a peak in the churning water and said, "Okay, Dustin, this wave has your name written all over it."

"I looked at it for one second and my heart dropped," Tester says. "It seemed as big as a skyscraper to my puny eight-year-old frame." But she pushed her fear aside and went for it. She immediately wiped out. Her board flew up in the air and spun around. Her leash wrapped around both ankles. She sank and couldn't kick to the surface. She knew she had to turn to free herself, so she guessed which direction. She was right. She wriggled out. She swam to the surface sputtering for air.

Despite that terrifying early experience, though, Tester kept at it. "I enjoyed using my body," she says. "It made me feel whole and grounded."

She soon needed the grounding. Her parents divorced shortly after she learned to surf. She spent summers in Maui with her dad and school years in California or Arkansas with her mom. The custody battles and cross-country relocations weren't easy. She spent every free weekend skimboarding on Makena Beach near her father's house. She surfed for hours on end, working off her anger, sprinting her legs off, racing into the water. She zoned out everyone on the beach and treated the waves as her stage for this sometimes violent, sometimes exhilarating dance.

She attended Prescott College. For her senior thesis, she designed a rite of passage program for adolescent girls. It used adventure education activities (like surfing) to help girls transform their body images. After a short stint working for a camp in North Carolina after school, she started Maui Surfer Girls to turn that thesis into reality. If she loved surfing as much as she loved living, she decided, she would be happiest making her living in the surf. So she made the choice to make self-actualization her top priority.

It wasn't easy. It was a "major leap of faith," she says. "Scarier than diving off Black Rock." She put her entire savings from her camp job down as a deposit on renting a few cabins near the beach for the next summer. Then, a few weeks later, she fractured her ankle in a climbing accident. After surgery, she wound up needing crutches for months. The possibility existed that she wouldn't even be able to surf come summer.

The injury did heal, over time. But three months before camp was to start, she faced the next scary-looking wave: low demand. Only six campers had signed up. Her father, usually her biggest supporter, advised her to bail out lest she wind up with her ankles hog-tied to the metaphorical board of a failing business. She could still get her deposit back at that point.

She ignored him and forged ahead. She watched the start date roll closer.

Then, a month before camp started, she got a grant from the University of Hawaii that paid for scholarships for six underprivileged girls to attend. More registrations flooded in at the last minute. She ended up with 17 campers for the first session of Maui Surfer Girls, enough to make the camp worthwhile. "That taught me to trust my gut and hold on tight for the ride," she says.

Now, Maui Surfer Girls brings dozens of campers to the islands every summer. The girls learn to surf, and keep journals as they live in their cabins on the beach. They get to know their bodies as functional objects, not simply decorative objects for others to see and judge. "I've watched girls grow up through my program and become very competent surfers and confident young women," Tester says.

Most campers figure out how to stand up and ride a wave after a day or two. A few years ago, though, one camper with a scoliosis-bent back and a troubled background couldn't stand on her board after a week of practice. She grew frustrated and wanted to quit. Tester coached her to tune out everything else. She was not to compare herself to others. They didn't matter. She would be able to surf someday, she told the girl, and that's all she needed to know. The girl agreed to keep trying.

She focused. She kept falling. But finally, as camp drew to a close, she figured out how to ride a wave. As soon as she stood up on that surfboard and kept her balance, she fell in love. She got so hooked that she found scholarships to come back to Maui Surfer Girls year after year, and she now works for Tester. She's gained a reputation as a crazy wave charger, dashing into walls of water twice her height. Everyone on the beach stares with their mouths open. Tester smiles as she sees where these baby steps led her protégé. "I'm so thankful," she says. How could she not be? *She does what she loves. She changes young women's lives. She works on the beach.* "I look around and think, 'Can you believe this is my office?' I pinch myself every summer when the campers come."

Job security is nice. So are steady paychecks. But there's no substitute for the joy that Tester feels when her charges pump their fists in the air after a good ride.

If you think that, too, then remember: when you are young, especially if you are looking after only yourself, you don't need to meet your needs in the usual order. You can zone out the middle levels of the hierarchy as you perform on your own rolling, splashing stage.

That's the choice Tester made. It's the choice all Grindhoppers make. If you build a career doing what you love, what makes you whole, according to your authentic vision, little else matters. Your life sparkles like the sun on Hawaii's waves.

THE GRINDHOPPING GIST

The seven Grindhopping Guidelines can help ambitious, impatient young people build rewarding careers without paying their dues. If you're really impatient, here's the cheat sheet version:

1. Always Be Your Own Boss

Grindhoppers are not willing to compromise their vision of the ideal career and the ideal life for long. When you're a Grindhopper, you run the show, just like a boss would. You also allow yourself no excuses for not doing everything you can to achieve that ideal, just as a boss would allow you no excuses. So how do you design your own show? To choose a career, Grindhoppers ask, "What do I love to do so much that I'd do it for free?" Then they ask, "How can I get people to pay me to do that?" For the latter, ask what needs people have and how you can meet those needs in a low-cost way that gets the cash register ringing quickly. Once you figure out your career, you need to understand that you alone are responsible for shaping that career and holding yourself to the to-do list. Grindhoppers are phenomenally disciplined. They exercise this discipline in four key ways: they don't rely on external rewards for motivation, they work hard even if no one notices, they don't rely on any one revenue stream, and they are frugal to a fault.

2. Know Where You're Going

Grindhoppers may not like the "G word" (goals), but they think about the future constantly. Not only do they think about the future, they ask what concrete steps they can take to get there. To build a career outside the grind, ask, "What can I do in the next day, week, month, year, and decade to achieve my big career goals?" Then evaluate all your decisions based on whether the results will get you closer to where you're going. Some Grindhoppers set strict goals for themselves. Others prefer to keep themselves on track with frequent gut checks. They ask, "Is there anything in my life I'm not happy with? If so, what is that, and how can I change it?" Then they act on that information.

3. Recalculate Risk

Grindhopping requires you to get comfortable with being uncomfortable. So Grindhoppers learn to evaluate risk differently from the way other people do. They realize that the risks of *not* pursuing a big goal can be as big as the risks of stretching themselves. They figure out what rock bottom would look like and ask if they're willing to deal with that if the worst happens. Then they focus on the upsides of risk, while hedging against the downsides. Grindhoppers also realize that fewer small business ventures fail than people claim, and that when you're young, the risks of failure are relative. You can always start over. And you might succeed, too. If you do, the upsides—from money to work-life flexibility—can be pretty sweet.

4. Think Projects, Not Jobs

We live in the Craig's List Economy these days. The labor market is becoming as flexible as the world's capital markets, and that's a good thing. Grindhoppers who flourish in this new economy have projects, not jobs. They are always chasing a dream project, and they are always thinking about the next dream project while they're working on the current one. They take on smaller projects to support themselves between big projects. They choose these smaller projects by asking of each one, "Is the project close to my heart?" Then they ask, "Do I respect the people I'll be working with?" and "Will this project help me in the long run?" Even when Grindhoppers moonlight to pay the bills, they make sure that these pay-the-bills projects keep them on track for landing dream projects someday.

5. Seek to Be Judged on Results (and Deliver Them)

Grindhoppers have a deep interest in quality. It's the one arena in which microenterprises can compete. They also have little patience with the face-time culture that infects so many offices. They seek out situations where people don't care so much about face time or age, and instead judge the Grindhoppers on what they can do. Grindhoppers in creative fields seek to improve their quality constantly by playing with their crafts, doing a lot of whatever it is they do best, evaluating other people's work, and learning from criticism of their products. Grindhoppers in relationship-based fields ask what needs their clients have, and then ask, "How can I show them that I am the right person to meet those needs?" All Grindhoppers understand that when you're young, you have to both overpromise and overdeliver in order to wow the people you work with. If you do wow them, though, you're set. You'll never have to hustle for work again.

6. Everything Is Negotiable

Grindhoppers learn to negotiate for money, but that's not all they negotiate. They also challenge widely held assumptions about the way the real world works. For instance, they don't believe that you have to pay your dues to reach positions of authority. Grindhoppers create their own training, without anyone deeming them ready for it. They switch careers as they desire. They believe that you can do good deeds and make money at the same time. Grindhoppers know that if you hop out of the grind, you can hop back in by wowing your clients and then mentioning that you're looking for job opportunities. Grindhoppers also understand that work-life balance is for people who create their own rules, not just for people who play in the chit system where face time earns flexibility.

7. Cultivate a Network and a Nimble Mind

Networking has gotten a bad reputation, but since people are great sources of knowledge, knowing people is the best way to learn what you need to know once you're out of school. You needn't be a connector to work connections. Simply join existing networks. Join a small group in your industry, a small group that is not in your industry (like a softball team or church group), a big professional group, and a big nonindustry network like an alumni e-mail list. These four networks will help you maximize the potential of your contacts. Also, make sure you get to know well-connected people. Impress them and they will open doors for you. Read everything you can so that you learn constantly, and approach problems like you're a reporter on assignment. Figure out what you need to know, who has that information, and how you get it from them. Keep your mind sharp by using it whenever you get the chance.

NOW WHAT?

Are you ready to hop out of the grind? If you've already hopped, are you looking to meet other Grindhoppers who are encountering similar challenges and rewards? The Grindhopping Web site (www.Grindhopping.com) has forums and articles that will help you build a career without paying your dues. Learn:

- **What to do before you quit your job**

- **How to organize multiple projects**

- **How to set goals for yourself and your career**

- **How to score benefits once you leave the grind**

- **How to hire help when you need it**

- **How to negotiate and set rates**

- **Easy ways to market yourself and your services**

You can also read more in-depth profiles of the Grindhoppers in this book and other Grindhoppers I've met in my research. You can even share your own story if you'd like. If you've got a question, post it, and other Grindhoppers on the site's forums will help you answer it. Or at least they'll moan with you about the problem. Sometimes that's even more fun. I'll see you there.

—*Laura*

ACKNOWLEDGMENTS

This book would not have been possible without the generosity of the Grindhoppers who shared the details of their careers and lives with me. These young men and women are an inspiring and free-spirited bunch. My brain started buzzing every time I interviewed them. I'd ask for 15 minutes on the phone and wind up lingering over lunch for hours. When people love their lives and find meaning in their work, their joy is contagious. The Grindhoppers in this book shared their time because they wanted others to experience the same joy. For this, I am grateful. I am also grateful to friends new and old who opened their address books to suggest subjects. In particular, I'd like to thank my most prolific source finders: Marci Alboher, Raoul Bhavnani, Anthony Hong, Maren Lau, Ron Shah, Caroline Tiger, and Tim Van Hooser.

I am also grateful to *USA Today*'s Forum page editors, John Siniff, Glen Nishimura, and, until her recent retirement, Chris Collins, for running my 2004 column on the sanity of self-employment, on which this book is based, as well as my columns on white-collar sweatshops, frugal graduates, entrepreneur moms, and other topics that *Grindhopping* addresses. Some editors might have been wary of sticking a 20-something kid's musings on their pages, but the folks at *USA Today* haven't been. This relationship, now more than five years old, has helped me grow as a writer.

I am grateful to Laura Yorke, Carol Mann, and Will Sherlin, all of the Carol Mann Agency, for placing this book with McGraw-Hill. I am also grateful to Monica Bentley, formerly of McGraw-Hill, for taking a chance on my proposal and acquiring this book. Melissa Bonventre, the subsequent editor for this project at McGraw-Hill, gave great advice as she ushered *Grindhopping* through its various drafts. Thanks to Daina Penikas and Alice Manning for seeing the book through production.

My friend Christine Whelan, author of *Why Smart Men Marry Smart Women*, served as a great sounding board as I hammered out the proposal for *Grindhopping*. Paul Young did an excellent job building the Grindhopping Web site (www.Grindhopping.com); I am grateful to Catherine Hall for the lovely photos she took of me for the site and for general publicity. Thanks to the American Society of Journalists and Authors' NYC book group for listening to me drone through sections during the writing process.

Most of all, thanks to my husband, Michael Conway, who is my biggest fan. Everything I know about business that's actually accurate I learned from him. It's easy to be happy, I've discovered, if you find both work you love and a spouse who keeps life interesting. I've been blessed abundantly with both.

NOTES

Unless otherwise specified, all information about Grindhoppers'
lives and ventures are from interviews with the Grindhoppers them-
selves. Most of the cited reports and press releases can be found
online by searching for the name in the note; I have provided URLs
in circumstances where the information is more difficult to find
through a simple search.

CARVING YOUR OWN CAREER PATH

7 "Chris Anderson, editor-in-chief of *Wired* magazine": see his discussion of this concept at www.thelongtail.com, and in Chris Anderson, *The Long Tail: Why the Future of Business Is Selling Less of More* (New York: Hyperion, 2006).

9 "'Trainees,' Whyte writes of young workers": William H. Whyte, *The Organization Man* (Garden City, NY: Doubleday, 1957), first printed by Simon & Schuster in 1956. Trainee quote is p. 145.

9 "The typical young Organization Man": Whyte, p. 122.

9 "In the meantime, the man companies decide they need": Whyte, p. 152.

9 "After some thought, a few trainees said . . ." : ibid.

9 "'I would sacrifice brilliance . . .'": ibid.

9 "In *Winning*, he talks about James": Jack Welch with Suzy Welch, *Winning* (New York: HarperBusiness, 2005), pp. 283–285.

10 "'It just might be that the source of your problem . . .'": Welch, p. 303.

10 "Yes, Welch tells us, there are no 'shortcuts'": Welch, p. 277 (the chapter's title is "Getting Promoted: Sorry, No Shortcuts").

10 "'Be loyal to the company and the company will be loyal to you.'": Whyte, p. 143.

10 "In 2001, for instance, *USA Today* fired . . .": For one account of this tale, see Kathryn S. Wenner, "Blue Christmas," *American Journalism Review*, January/February 2002. Available online at http://www.ajr.org/Article.asp?id=2435.

11   "I was reminded of this in a recent *Time* magazine profile of Best Buy": Jyoti Thottam, "Reworking Work," *Time*, July 25, 2005, pp. 50–55.

12   "I see evidence of the split in Barbara Ehrenreich's book": Barbara Ehrenreich, *Bait and Switch: The (Futile) Pursuit of the American Dream* (New York: Metropolitan Books, 2005).

12   "When I wrote a piece called 'The Sanity of Self-Employment,'": Laura Vanderkam, "The Sanity of Self-Employment," *USA Today*, July 12, 2004.

13   "The National Association for the Self-Employed reports that": National Association for the Self-Employed, "Frequently Asked Questions," available at http://news.nase.org/nase_about/FAQ.asp.

13   "A recent NASE survey found that 13.9 percent": Correspondence with Katy Dyer, public affairs associate, NASE, February 13, 2006. She reports that 1.6 percent of the membership is under 25, and 12.3 percent is between 25 and 34 years old.

13   "Bureau of Labor Statistics figures show that about 10 million Americans": The official number in February 2005 was 10.3 million. See, for example, BLS, "Contingent and Alternative Employment Arrangements, February 2005," July 27, 2005, available at http://www.bls.gov/news.release/conemp.nro.htm. For the incorporated number, Steven Hipple, in "Self-Employment in the United States," *Monthly Labor Review*, July 2004, notes that rates of incorporated self-employed persons have ranged from 3.2 to 3.6 percent of the labor force since 1994. With a labor force of roughly 150 million people, that would be 4.8 million to 5.4 million. Daniel Pink (see the following citation) uses 4 million.

13   "Daniel Pink, author of *Free Agent Nation*": Daniel Pink, *Free Agent Nation* (New York: Warner Books, 2002), p. 42.

15   "We are *Strapped*, to quote one recent title": Tamara Draut, *Strapped: Why America's 20- and 30-Somethings Can't Get Ahead* (New York: Doubleday, 2005).

15   "We are *Generation Debt*, to quote another": Anya Kamenetz, *Generation Debt: Why Now Is a Terrible Time to Be Young* (New York: Riverhead, 2006).

15   "We are caught up in a *Quarterlife Crisis*": Alexandra Robbins and Abby Wilner, *Quarterlife Crisis: The Unique Challenges of Life in Your Twenties* (New York: Tarcher/ Putnam, 2001).

16   "The day I visited, a *Wall Street Journal* article": Ilan Brat, "A Company's Threat: Quit Smoking or Leave," *Wall Street Journal*, December 21, 2005.

GRINDHOPPING GUIDELINE 1: ALWAYS BE YOUR OWN BOSS

22   "As a unified public relations force": Jean Scheidnes, "Austin Craft Mafia Conquers Cable with New Show," *Austin American-Statesman*, March 30, 2006.

23   "We hear that to find the right job, in Jack Welch's words,": Jack Welch with Suzy Welch, *Winning* (New York: HarperBusiness, 2005), p. 256.

24   "I shivered when I read a story in a book called *Career Bliss*": Joanne Gordon, *Career Bliss* (New York: Ballantine Books, 2006), pp. 29–31.

25   "On the other hand, as Peter Lynch showed in his 1993 book": Peter Lynch with John Rothchild, *Beating the Street* (New York: Simon & Schuster, 1993), pp. 26–35. The "inexplicable venture" quote is p. 27.

26   "Then they write testimonials saying": VocationVacations rotates through different testimonials on the site. For more info, see www.vocationvacations.com.

26   "Gordon's *Career Bliss* notes": Gordon, pp. 29–31.

27   "One of the most interesting is that of Elizabeth Murray": Patricia Cleary, *Elizabeth Murray: A Woman's Pursuit of Independence in Eighteenth-Century America* (Amherst, MA: University of Massachusetts Press, 2000).

28   "She took out ads in the Boston newspaper": Cleary, p. 56. (She reprints this ad from the Massachusetts Historical Society, Boston. The ad dates from ca. 1749.)

28   "When sales were thin at the store": Cleary, pp. 58 and 63.

28   ". . . so well that Murray had one of her husbands sign a prenuptial agreement": Cleary, p. 85.

28   "According to Cleary, Murray was one of at least 90": Cleary, p. 46.

28   "'As partners or patrons of one another's businesses . . .'": Cleary, p. 74.

28   "One woman even left her estate to another": ibid.

30   "North American corporate acquisitions": Tim Reason, "A High-water Mark?" *CFO Magazine*, January 1, 2006.

30   "I'd read about a sand-sculpture business": Barbara J. Winter, *Making a Living without a Job* (New York: Bantam Books, 1993), p. 46.

35   "Then there's another school of thought, best expressed": Alfie Kohn, *Punished by Rewards: The Trouble with Gold Stars, Incentive Plans, A's, Praise, and Other Bribes* (Boston: Houghton Mifflin, 1993).

35   "Several top business schools, for instance, don't": See "Campus Confidential," *BusinessWeek*, September 12, 2005.

36   "The 2006 *Statistical Abstract*": Census Bureau, *Statistical Abstract of the United States*," http://www.census.gov/prod/2005pubs/06statab/labor.pdf (Table 590). These figures go through summer 2005.

36   "I first interviewed this Chicago-area Grindhopper": Laura Vanderkam, "White-Collar Sweatshops Batter Young Workers," *USA Today*, November 26, 2002.

38   "It's easier to assume that your current gig or gigs will always be there: Spencer Johnson's *Who Moved My Cheese?* (New York: Putnam, 1998) spent years on the best-seller list. The tales of people being forced to read it at work come from Thomas Frank, *One Market under God* (New York: Anchor Books, 2000), in his updated afterword on p. 368.

38   "More than half of Americans": MetLife, "The MetLife Study of Employee Benefits Trends," November 2003, p. 5.

39   "According to the Bureau of Economic Analysis": Bureau of Economic Analysis, U.S. Department of Commerce, "Personal Income and Outlays: February 2006," March 31, 2006.

39   "One of the reasons this rate has fallen from 8 to 10 percent": For a historical chart, see the Federal Reserve Bank of San Francisco's

Economic Letter, "What's Behind the Low U.S. Personal Saving Rate?" March 29, 2002, available at http://www.frbsf.org/publications/economics/letter/2002/el2002-09.html.

39   "That's why the Federal Reserve calculates": Federal Reserve, "Consumer Credit," (updates monthly; this figure was correct as of April 7, 2006) available at http://www.federalreserve.gov/releases/g19/current/default.htm. I'm using a rough figure for the number of households in the United States (100 million).

39   "'Lyndsey graduated from college in 2000 . . .'": M. P. Dunleavey, "Young, Carefree . . . and Deep in Debt," *MSN Money*, available at http://moneycentral.msn.com/content/CollegeandFamily/Moneyin your20s/P105691.asp.

39   "Demos, a progressive think tank, tried to lobby": Tamara Draut and Javier Silva, "Generation Broke: The Growth of Debt among Young Americans," Demos, October 2004. Student loans are cited on p. 7, real wages on p. 5. The sample budget is on p. 6.

40   "Yet somehow the Demos figures": I've found this $34 figure cited in the *St. Petersburg Times* and in a piece distributed by Knight Ridder.

41   "The average length of unemployment is four to five months": Bureau of Labor Statistics, "Unemployed Persons by Duration of Unemployment," Table A-9 in the monthly "Employment Situation" release, available at http://www.bls.gov/news.release/empsit.t09.htm. This site updates monthly. For the past year, as of April 2006, it's hovered between 16 and 20 weeks.

43   "Professor Robert Emmons at the University of California–Davis": For an overview of the research, see Robert A. Emmons and Michael E. McCullough, "Highlights from the Research Project on Gratitude and Thankfulness," available at http://psychology.ucdavis.edu/labs/emmons/.

GRINDHOPPING GUIDELINE 2: KNOW WHERE YOU'RE GOING

45   "Indeed, Richard Wiseman, a British psychologist": Richard Wiseman, *The Luck Factor: Changing Your Luck, Changing Your Life—The Four Essential Principles* (New York: Miramax Books, 2003).

50   "A June 2005 survey from the Hudson Highland Group": The Hudson Employment Index, "Workers Satisfied with Compensation; Unsure

about Performance Reviews," June 15. 2005. Available at http://www.hudson-index.com/node.asp?SID=4561.

50   "Others stumble into an angst-ridden state": Alexandra Robbins and Abby Wilner, *Quarterlife Crisis: The Unique Challenges of Life in Your Twenties* (New York: Tarcher/Putnam, 2001), and Lia Macko and Kerry Rubin, *Midlife Crisis at 30: How the Stakes Have Changed for a New Generation—and What to Do About It* (New York: Rodale Books, 2004).

52   "My friend Christine, a writer, uses a program called Stickies": to download this program, visit http://www.zhornsoftware.co.uk/stickies/.

56   "To add insult to injury": see Sue Hendrikson's biography at http://sue-hendrickson.net/biography.asp.

GRINDHOPPING GUIDELINE 3: RECALCULATE RISK

61   "Harland Sanders did not have an easy or comfortable life": These dates and tales come from the official KFC biography of Sanders, available at http:// www.kfc.com/about/colonel.htm. The quote is copied from the plaque in the Corbin, Kentucky, KFC.

67   "A recent *BusinessWeek* article, however, noted": Lindsey Gerdes, "You Have 20 Minutes to Surf. Go," *BusinessWeek*, December 26, 2005, p. 16.

67   "In 2005, the California Supreme Court found itself": details of this case have been widely reported. For one account, see Mike McKee, "Calif. Justices See Retaliation in Make-Up Case," *The Recorder*, August 15, 2005.

68   "Many of the items on outplacement firm Challenger, Gray & Christmas's list": Challenger, Gray & Christmas, Inc., "The Most Unbelievable Workplace Events of 2005," available at www.challengergray.com/press%20releases/2005%20Top%20Unbelievable%20Events.pdf .

69   "Interview Gen-X workers who are worried about layoffs": this quote from Tulgan is from an interview. See the citation for his book in the Grindhopping Guideline 5 notes.

69   "You've probably seen the statistic floating around that": Researching this book, I've been amazed at how many people quoted

this statistic to me, even though it's inaccurate. If you do an Internet search on this statistic, you'll find a number of Web sites quoting it verbatim. It is false; see the following note.

69   "According to a study by Amy E. Knaup": Amy E. Knaup, "Survival and Longevity in the Business Employment Dynamics Database," *Monthly Labor Review*, Vol. 128, No. 5, May 2005, pp. 50–56. Available online at http://www.bls.gov/opub/mlr/2005/05/ressum.pdf.

69   "There were 576,200 small business closures in 2004": Small Business Administration, Office of Advocacy, "Frequently Asked Questions," citing Bureau of the Census, Department of Labor, and Administrative Office of the U.S. Courts data, available at http://www.sba.gov/advo/stats/sbfaq.pdf.

70   "You can see the fast fall in the 2001 documentary": *Startup.com* (2001), directed by Chris Hegedus and Jehane Noujaim, produced by Noujaim Films and Pennebaker Hegedus Films.

70   "In 2000, you needed a paper net worth": "You Can't Tell the Rich Kids without a Scorecard," *Fortune*, September 18, 2000, pp. 115–118. The 2004 list is in the September 20, 2004, issue.

71   "Ellen Parlapiano and Patricia Cobe": Ellen Parlapiano and Patricia Cobe, *Mompreneurs* (New York: Berkley Publishing Group, 1996). See also *Mompreneurs Online* (New York: Perigee Books, 2001).

72   "He speaks at various entrepreneurship conferences": For a current biography of Kaleil Isaza Tuzman, please see www.kaleil.com. For the *Reader's Digest* piece, see "The American Dream," *Reader's Digest*, May 2004, p. 69. The Entrepreneur's Success Kit was released by St. Martin's Press in 2005.

75   "Two 30-something guys named Larry and Sergey": Kevin J. Delaney, J. Lynn Lunsford, and Mark Maremont, "Google Duo's New Jet Is a Boeing 767-200," *Wall Street Journal*, November 4, 2005. Google stock closed over $400 on November 17, 2005.

75   "The National Association for the Self-Employed reports that": National Association for the Self-Employed, "Who Are the Self-Employed?" cites the March 1997 Current Population Survey from the Census Bureau. Available at http://news.nase.org/news/selfemployed.asp.

75   "Two-thirds of the high-net-worth individuals that Thomas Stanley": Thomas J. Stanley and William D. Danko, *The Millionaire Next Door* (New York: Pocket Books, 1998), p. 8 in paperback.

76   "The Census Bureau's 1997 Current Population Survey": National Association for the Self-Employed, ibid.

76   "In a recent Freelancers Union study of New York City": Freelancers Union, "The Rise of the Freelance Class," 2005.

GRINDHOPPING GUIDELINE 4: THINK PROJECTS, NOT JOBS

81   "They cite stats like a February 2005 study": Bureau of Labor Statistics, "Contingent and Alternative Employment Arrangements, February 2005," released July 27, 2005, available at http://www.bls.gov/news.release/conemp.nro.htm. The statistics in the next two paragraphs are also from this study.

87   "From *Cooking Light*, 'The pumpkin is a master of disguise. . . .'": Sarah Lacamoire, "Prompt Pumpkin," *Cooking Light*, November 2003.

87   "From the *Boston Globe*, 'If the Scotch whisky industry . . .'": Sarah Lacamoire, "The Spirit of Scotland: Scotch Whisky," *Boston Globe*, May 29, 2005.

GRINDHOPPING GUIDELINE 5: SEEK TO BE JUDGED ON RESULTS (AND DELIVER THEM)

98   "She's since done the art for over a dozen books": Phil Bildner (illutrated by LeUyen Pham), *Twenty-One Elephants* (New York: Simon & Schuster Children's Books, 2004).

99   "*Booklist* praised it, noting": Karin Snelson, "Twenty-One Elephants," *Booklist*, October 1, 2004, p. 332.

99   "Pham's first solo effort": LeUyen Pham, *Big Sister, Little Sister* (New York: Hyperion, 2005).

99   "A 2005 Families and Work Institute survey found": Families and Work Institute, "2005 National Study of Employers," October, 2005, Highlights of Findings, p. 4.

100   "Although 29 percent of employees in another Families and Work Institute survey: Families and Work Institute, "Overwork in America: When the Way We Work Becomes Too Much," March, 2005, Executive Summary, p. 4.

100   "A 2005 *Harvard Business Review* study": Sylvia Ann Hewlett and Carolyn Buck Luce, "Off-Ramps and On-Ramps: Keeping Talented Women on the Road to Success," *Harvard Business Review*, Vol. 83, No. 3, March 2005.

100   "A July 2005 report from the Department of Labor": Bureau of Labor Statistics, "Workers on Flexible and Shift Schedules in May 2004 Summary," July 1, 2005, available at http://www.bls.gov/news.release/flex.nro.htm. This summary offers percentages for its historical tables, not raw numbers. The numbers for 2001 were extrapolated in Stephanie Armour, "Fewer Working Flex-time Hours, Report Says," *USA Today*, July 24, 2005.

100   "A 2005 Society for Human Resource Management": Society for Human Resource Management, "2005 Benefits Survey Report," June 2005. Also see citation from *USA Today* in previous note.

100   "Indeed, for all the talk about judging people on results": The Hudson Employment Index, "Workers Satisfied with Compensation; Unsure about Performance Reviews," June 15, 2005.

101   "My husband brings home his McKinsey staff papers": Tsun-yan Hsieh, "The Zen of Organization: A Perspective for the Disciplined Practitioner," McKinsey Staff Paper No. 63, December 2005, p. 3.

101   "As Bruce Tulgan, author of *Winning the Talent Wars*, explains it": Bruce Tulgan, *Winning the Talent Wars* (New York: W.W. Norton & Company, 2001), p. 93.

101   "A 2002 *Financial Times* investigation found that": Ien Cheng, "The Barons of Bankruptcy," *Financial Times*, July 31- August 2, 2002.

GRINDHOPPING GUIDELINE 6: EVERYTHING IS NEGOTIABLE

113   "Good luck doing that in a corporation that hires": National Association of Colleges and Employers, "High Starting Salaries Show Competition Heating up for New College Grads," April 6, 2006.

114   "Women in particular, according to": Linda Babcock and Sara Laschever, *Women Don't Ask* (Princeton, NJ: Princeton University Press, 2003), p. 114.

121   ". . . a magazine that *The Nation* later described as 'a chocolate sampler for the mind'": Amy Wilentz, "In Cold Type," *The Nation*, January 13, 2003.

122 "Haskell would like to have *Topic* win": for quote from David Remnick and the awards Topic has won, see http://www.topicmag.com/page.php?page=about.

122 "A 2004 University of Phoenix survey": University of Phoenix, "A University of Phoenix Study Examines Career Moves for Working Adults," September 7, 2004.

123 "One of its books on a subject near to his heart": Kathleen Cushman, Edward Miller, and Lawrence G. Anderson, *How to Produce a Small Newspaper: A Guide for Independent Journalists* (Harvard, MA: Harvard Common Press, 1978).

124 "The Modern Language Association counted": statistics from Rosemary Feal, executive director of the MLA, in correspondence May 6, 2003.

124 "One 1999 study found that only 53 percent": Maresi Nerad and Joseph Cerny, "PhDs Ten Years Later," 1999, printed in *ADE Bulletin* 124 (Winter 2000), pp. 43–55 as "From Rumors to Facts: Career Outcomes of English PhDs." Available online at http://www.mla.org/ade/bulletin/N124/124043.htm. For more discussion of the 8 percent at Carnegie Research I institutions, see the "From the Editor" discussion by David Laurence, pp. 1–4, available online at http://www.mla.org/ade/bulletin/ n124/124001.htm.

125 "Each year students at over 100 colleges sign": see http://www.graduationpledge.org/schools.html for a list of schools at the Graduation Pledge Alliance Web site, which gives the wording of the pledge.

126 "According to Charity Navigator": see the listing on the Red Cross at www.charitynavigator.org. This figure is for the fiscal year ending in June, 2004. Charity Navigator updates its figures on the Web site as non-profits release their new annual reports, so the figure currently shown may be different.

126 "Reynold Levy, president of Lincoln Center": see the listing on Lincoln Center at www.charitynavigator.org. This figure is for the fiscal year ending in June, 2004; please see the discussion of Charity Navigator's updates in the previous note.

126 "According to Charity Navigator, Hale House: also at www.charitynavigator.org; please see the discussion in the previous note.

126 "Maybe that's because donors are still sore": see New York State's Office of the Attorney General, "Former Hale House Director Pleads Guilty to Felony Charges Involving the Misappropriation of Charitable Funds," July 3, 2002.

127 "The FDA forbids organizations from importing drugs": Illinois allows citizens to buy drugs from Canada, Ireland, and elsewhere through the site http://www.i-saverx.net/. Residents of Kansas, Wisconsin, Vermont, and Missouri can also order through this site.

130 "In 2002, Sylvia Ann Hewlett's book": Sylvia Ann Hewlett, *Creating a Life: Professional Women and the Quest for Children* (New York: Miramax Books, 2002), p. 42.

130 "Former Harvard President Larry Summers fanned the flames": Lawrence H. Summers, "Remarks at NBER Conference on Diversifying the Science & Engineering Workforce," January 14, 2005.

130 "Jack Welch notes in *Winning* that": Jack Welch with Suzy Welch, *Winning* (New York: HarperBusiness, 2005), p. 321.

130 ". . . the rise in the number of stay-at-home moms": This statistic is based on the report "America's Families and Living Arrangements: 2003" from the Census Bureau. It is available in Table 5 at www.census.gov/prod/2004pubs/p20-553.pdf. The 4.5 million in 1994 is based on Sharon Jayson, "Census: 5.4 Million Mothers Are Choosing to Stay at Home," *USA Today*, December 1, 2004, p. 3A.

130 "As Yale student Cynthia Liu": Louise Story, "Many Women at Elite Colleges Set Career Path to Motherhood," *New York Times*, September 20, 2005, p. A1.

130 "The number of women-owned businesses rose": Center for Women's Business Research, "Top Facts about Women-Owned Businesses," available at http://www.womensbusinessresearch.org/topfacts.html.

GRINDHOPPING GUIDELINE 7: CULTIVATE A NETWORK AND A NIMBLE MIND

134 "But for me, knowing these truths about myself": Keith Ferrazzi with Tahl Raz, *Never Eat Alone* (New York: Doubleday, 2005).

134 "Jeffrey Meshel's new book on networking": Jeffrey W. Meshel with Douglas Garr, *One Phone Call Away* (New York: Portfolio, 2005). The jewelry story is on pp. 94–96.

134   "Malcolm Gladwell, in *The Tipping Point*: Malcolm Gladwell, *The Tipping Point* (New York: Back Bay Books, 2002). "Connectors" are introduced on p. 38.

DEALING WITH THE DOWNSIDES

152   "When I lived in Washington, D.C.": The health insurance market is constantly shifting. I bought my policy through a Web site www.TemporaryInsurance.com, which is currently run by a company called Assurant Health. Check www.eHealthInsurance.com for long-term individual policies, or simply Google "health insurance." TONIK health plans are available in some states at www.tonikhealth.com. As self-employment rates rise, the market for individual policies expands. Just remember, health insurance is rarely cheap. If you find a too-good-to-be-true policy (e.g., "Health Insurance for $10 a Month!"), it's probably a scam.

153   "I checked the Web site for current New York rates": See http://www.workingtoday.org/ productsservices/healthdental.php/. These rates may change by the time you're reading this.

153   "Google, according to a recent *Time* magazine profile": Adi Ignatius, "In Search of the Real Google," *Time*, February 20, 2006, p. 43.

161   "This 'hierarchy of needs' phrase comes from Abraham Maslow": He first laid out this theory in Abraham Maslow, "A Theory of Human Motivation." *Psychological Review*, Vol. 50, 1943, pp. 370–396 and subsequently elaborated on it.

162   "The French youth unemployment rate is currently 23 percent": "A Tale of Two Frances," *Economist*, April 1, 2006, p. 22.

162   "A late 2005 Right Management Consultants survey found that": Right Management Consultants, "Worker Confidence Levels Rise in 13 Countries, But Drop in 5 . . .," November 15, 2005. The company does a Career Confidence Index study twice a year; results can be downloaded from http://www.right.com/global/newsroom/cci.asp.

162   "One recent OfficeTeam survey found that 71 percent of employees": OfficeTeam, "Passing the Buck: Survey Reveals Most Workers Wouldn't Want to Be Boss," October 4, 2005.

162   "As William H. Whyte wrote in *The Organization Man*": William H. Whyte, *The Organization Man* (Garden City, NY: Doubleday, 1957), first printed by Simon & Schuster in 1956, p. 145.

162   "A 2005 Maritz poll found that only 20 percent of workers": Maritz, "Employee Outlook on Company Growth Significantly More Positive than Last Year," May 24, 2005.

164   ". . . after reading an eye-popping article": Jeffrey McCracken, "Detroit's Symbol of Dysfunction: Paying Employees Not to Work," *Wall Street Journal*, March 1, 2006.

INDEX

ABOUT THE AUTHOR

Laura Vanderkam writes columns for *USA TODAY* as a member of that paper's Board of Contributors, and is a contributing editor at *Reader's Digest*. She is the coauthor, with Jan and Bob Davidson, of *Genius Denied: How to Stop Wasting Our Brightest Young Minds* (Simon & Schuster, 2004) and is coauthor, with Dr. David Clayton, of *The Healthy Guide to Unhealthy Living: How to Survive Your Bad Habits* (Simon & Schuster, 2006). She lives with her husband, Michael Conway, in New York City.